Lunch Notes

Linda Rose

Your Choices become your Habits,
Your Habits become your Character

TATE PUBLISHING & *Enterprises*

Published by Tate Publishing & Enterprises, LLC
127 E. Trade Center Terrace | Mustang, Oklahoma 73064 USA
1.888.361.9473 | www.tatepublishing.com

Tate Publishing is committed to excellence in the publishing industry. The company reflects the philosophy established by the founders, based on Psalm 68:11,
"The Lord gave the word and great was the company of those who published it."

Published in the United States of America

ISBN: 978-1-60462-984-2
1. Christian Living: Relationships: Parenting
2. Religion: Christianity: Christian Life: Parenting
3. Family Relationships: Parenting
08.04.29

This book is dedicated to my loving family:
my husband, Roger, and our three daughters,
Jessica, Sarah, and Emily.
I will cherish the memories that we
have had together always.

Foreword by
Bobbye Rankin

The author of the book you are about to read is a self-proclaimed "memory fanatic"! Linda Rose's crystal-clear vision of having a godly, joyful family has been fueled by a burning passion to instill God's Word into the lives of her three daughters. Along with her wonderful husband, Roger, Linda's unwavering devotion to God and family has begun a spiritual legacy that will bear fruit for generations to come.

Christian parents find themselves challenged as never before as they seek to nurture their children in a contemporary society alien to godly principles. Parent-child interaction is impacted by demanding schedules and a plethora of activities that supersede family time. Peer pressure begins at an early age and tends to escalate steadily in adolescence. The latest fashions, electronic gadgets, and Internet capabilities are seen as status symbols that define one's contentment and worth. How can children in today's culture grow up confident and equipped to resist the deceptive influences of worldly values? How do parents most effectively guide their children to base their decisions on the Word of God?

In *Lunch Notes*, Linda shares a biblical pattern of parenting and family life that has resulted in three daughters who are devoted to serving God. Christ-centered, biblical principles were ingrained in their family not as an irrelevant, pious imposition, but as vibrant truth—fun and irresistible! Fresh, creative ideas, from daily Scripture notes of encouragement to parties and excursions, will give parents practical tools as they guide children through challenging, developmental years. Linda's message is that prayer without ceasing, the authority of God's Word and His powerful presence, coupled with parental unconditional love and time, are paramount in training young lives to love the Lord with all their heart, mind, and soul. Enjoy, envision, learn, and be blessed as you take this exciting, creative journey with the Rose family!

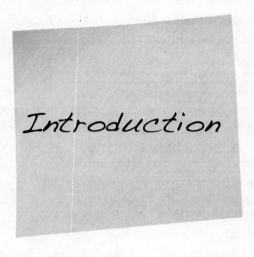

Introduction

I have been happily married for thirty-one years to Roger, a wonderful godly man. Our marriage and family is special because of the great work that God has done in our lives. Family life can be so extraordinary. We deliberately lived in such a way that God's grace could be evident. These ideas and lunch notes come from our overwhelming desire to create a home with our three daughters that brought honor to the Lord. Not just a group of people who lived together with the same last name, but a caring relationship with others built on principles from God's Word. Home should be a haven of refuge, a shelter from the storm. My husband's desire, along with mine, was to raise them up to be supportive of one another. Our goal became to teach our children more than attending church on Sunday; we wanted them to have an abundant life with Jesus Christ. Our motive was to teach them God's

Word, and how to use it on an everyday basis. It must be deliberate. We can be ready for the spectacular events that demand our attention, but the annoying everyday circumstances can leave us unhinged.

Maybe you are weary, or perhaps exhausted. Be encouraged. God's Word can teach us how to handle unfortunate situations and how to be ready when confronted with conditions that are out of our control. It is during the mundane that we are caught off guard. It is in these times that we must remember that God's love is not put away for Easter and Christmas, or even Sundays. He loves and cares for us every single minute of every day. "How great is the love the Father has lavished on us that we should be called the children of God and that is what we are..." (1 John 3:1).

God has lavished me with his love. Through Jesus, his grace and mercy has changed my destiny. Because of his death on the cross I now have an eternal home. I am always welcome because I will always be his child. Maybe you have a dream of a close family where peace dwells and relationships flourish. With God's Word as our source and some helpful ideas to get you started you can begin to make that dream a reality.

Chapter 1

Let me admit from the beginning that I am a "memory fanatic." I wanted lots of special moments, and I also wanted my children to look back on their lives at home as a special time. My husband could talk for hours about his brother, his sisters, and his parents. The stories were endless of vacations, campouts, and special family gatherings. My family life was not like that, and I had a void to fill. I had a yearning to fill every moment of my children's lives with meaning and preparation for the future. By doing this, I could help to equip them for the time when they would leave home, and also teach them the love of Christ in an every day way.

I attacked motherhood with all the tenacity of a pit-bull. I don't mean that I enjoyed every single day of the preschool years, but I had goals and dreams to fulfill. I memorized Proverbs 31 and went to work. Every single day wasn't a picnic, and the younger your children are the harder it is, but you have to be steadfast in your task. As believers in Jesus Christ we have to keep our focus steady and begin to take a stand for what counts. The guidelines for raising godly children are clearly defined in God's Word, Deuteronomy 6:4–9. As a couple that is exactly what my husband and I did. There was not a magic formula that we followed, we just opened God's Word and prayed for ideas.

The power of Christ to transform a life will always be a mystery to me. Especially as I look back on my own life. Our home life was often troubled, so I dreamed with expectancy that I might one day have a peaceful life. We were active in church, but I was confused about the concept of God's love. In fact, God's love seemed unattainable. The reason seemed obvious. God was not real.

After completing high school, I was awarded a grant to attend Oklahoma Baptist University. This was to be one of the first examples of God intervening in my life. As I entered dorm life and became acquainted with other girls, it was painful to see that my family life had been different than my peers. This left me bitter, angry, and ashamed. My parents became more and more distant and I began to realize that I was very alone.

God put people in my path to help and encourage me but trusting them proved very difficult. One girl encouraged me to go to God, but I had no interest. She begged me to go to church. Finally, I agreed to go once if she promised to never ask again. She agreed. That night, I asked Jesus into my heart to be my Savior. The next week I was baptized. I began meeting with a couple who taught me how to study the Bible. They were straightforward about areas of my life that needed immediate help. Although I had never been immoral and never took part in drinking or drugs, my actions and attitudes needed extensive adjustments. Because of their tireless support I made great strides in my personal life and my relationship with Christ.

I learned if I were the only person ever born, Jesus would have died on the cross just for me. He is a loving God who wants what is best for his children. His love is endless and amazing. He healed my hurts and gave me joy and hope for the future. To be his child was the most remarkable thing I have ever known. Since that time God has continued to reveal himself to me. The hurt and pain didn't go away suddenly, but he has been faithful, encouraging, guiding, and loving.

God expects us to use his Word to encompass every single minute of our day. Every moment of your child's life is a big deal. Teach them by your example how to apply God's Word to every area of life. Memories are made daily as you live out your regular routines. The difference is doing them with deliberate intention of shaping memories and establishing family relations. You just don't wake up one morning and have a great family. You build the foundation one moment at a time.

It is God's plan for you as a wife and mother to create an atmosphere of peace in your home. God has a special plan for each one of his children. As mothers it is our responsibility to equip them with whatever tools they need to be whatever God wants them to be. 1 Corinthians 2:9, "No eye has seen, no ear has heard, no mind can conceive what God has prepared for those who love him."

This tells us that God unmistakably has a plan for everyone and he has also prepared something for us. From the time our children start to walk, we are to be working ourselves out of a job. Yet at the same time, we are to be equipping them for dependence on and a relationship with the Almighty God. We must teach our children that family members are treated with the same respect as guest. There is a special bond with family that is hard work but worth the effort. Every day we encounter situations that are hard to handle. When our circumstances become difficult our families should work together to encourage and support each other. This will not happen naturally. However we can teach our children that they can overcome the hard times in victory. This is our job as parents and as followers of Jesus.

Many times we do not do extra things because we are too busy or tired. Another week passes and we have not made a dent in the relationships we crave most. We experience defeat and sadness. Possibly we do not even consider the different ways we can incorporate God's Word into our lives. The whole point of hiding God's Word in your heart is so that you can rely on it when you need it. Hopefully these ideas can be catalysts to help you visualize ways you can give God's Word to your children daily. Proverbs 19:20, "Listen to advice and accept instruction, and in the end you will be wise."

Our bathrooms are equipped with a small bulletin board. This is a sensible place to stick notes of encouragement or instruction since everyone goes there eventually. The bulletin board is simply one more place that you can tuck God's Word, or place a gentle reminder to do chores, maybe even an inspirational nugget of truth. You can put funny comics, cards, or just fun stickers. I try to put a short greeting or catchy theme for the week. At the start of each week, I replace it with a new thought. If family members have not spent time in God's Word, then at least it is right before their eyes several times a day. Nevertheless, if they are spending time in God's Word, there is nothing wrong with a short commercial. Some days when I am discouraged I have come to my bathroom and read a note of encouragement from one of my children or husband. When the intention is to show support for one another even a small note can change the dynamics of a relationship. The giver has shown kindness, given a surprise to the family member, and strengthened the bond of the family. This has been accomplished by simply taking the time to write, "I love you," on a piece of paper!

As believers, we are in a battle that we must take seriously. We must fight for the unity of our home and family. We must be forever faithful to the cause of Jesus Christ, and therefore, never desert our standard. But if they do not have a weapon they cannot fight and most certainly cannot win.

The pressures of raising a family in this world are overwhelming. As parents, we cannot do it alone. We must rely on God for strength and wisdom. The only normal that you can count on is that your home life will continually alter as your children grow, mature, and face unpredictable changes. God's Word is the only constant source of strength and power. Allow his presence to rule in your home. When the struggles and battles come remember, his power is made perfect in weakness. Then rely on his power to get you through. John 16:33, "I have told you these things so that in me you may have peace. In this world you will have trouble. But take heart! I have overcome the world."

As parents, you have the privilege of shaping your child's future. Make it count. Treasure each day. Don't be so caught up in the busyness of life that you miss living.

Make new memories and cherish old ones. Use the

gifts that God has given you to make your family life special and unique. When you encounter situations that you do not know how to handle, go to God's Word. There is no situation in this world that has not been covered in God's Word. James 1:5, "If any of you lacks wisdom, he should ask God, who gives generously to all without finding fault, and it will be given to him."

Chapter 2

The Tone of Your Home

Colossians 3:1–2, "Since, then, you have been raised with Christ, set your hearts on things above, where Christ is seated at the right hand of God. Set your minds on things above, not on earthly things."

As believers we still have to make a choice to serve God every day. In Mark 8, Jesus is speaking to his disciples (who had already made the choice to follow Christ) when he said, "You must deny yourself to follow me." That choice must be made every day and some days more than once. It is not enough for us to just know God's plan. We must make the choice to obey and follow him out of love and out of obedience. Mothers are easily distracted because we all desire to have nice homes, happy children, and content husbands. Yet the world continually calls to us through commercials, radio, and advertising. They are telling us that we must have nice homes, the latest model car, and the clothes from the right store. Still our Savior calls, "Follow me."

Nonetheless it is a matter of discipline and discipleship. The things that occupy our time and keep us full of activity might have redeemable qualities. But are these things getting us closer to the goal?

Experiencing God's presence in your home will have to be intentional. Consider playing audio music instead of the constant stimulation that television offers. Filter what you allow to come into your home, then reflect on what type of impression that makes on your family. I challenge you to play praise music or videos instead of TV in your home and see the difference. Keep in mind that Satan cannot dwell where Christ is.

Application:

As you begin to establish family traditions and unity, do not delude yourself by assuming that music and entertainment have no part in shaping attitudes and values. Look at the people you walk past daily. How many of them carry iPods, camera phones or Palm Pilots? Or add up the money you spend on DVDs, music CDs or movie tickets. This speaks volumes. If you have equipped your children with their own entertainment system you will be hard pressed to have much family time. Buying individual electronics for your children teaches them to live separate lives. If you give them their own equipment they never have to share or cooperate. Consider this, if your children go to their rooms to play with their technology, how can you spend time building unity? Make the hard choice now to spend time learning what your children watch, whom they admire, and who influences their thoughts. This is your God given responsibility. A change of this magnitude will be painful, and you should brace yourself for a battle. It is easier to change what you believe than it is to adjust your behavior to Scriptural principles. Remember 1 Corinthians 4:1-2, "So then, men ought to regard us as servants of Christ and as those entrusted with the secret things of God. Now it is required that those who have been given a trust must prove faithful."

Family Unity

Colossians 1:9-12, "We have not stopped praying for you, and asking God to fill you with the knowledge of his will through all spiritual wisdom and understanding, and we pray this in order that you may please God, being strengthened with all power according to his glorious might so that you may have great endurance and patience ..."

Pray for family unity. One night a week, as a couple, we pray only for our immediate family's needs. We pray specific scriptures for each other as believers. Our prayer for our family is one that says:

Dear Father, Help us to depend on one another. Encourage us to love the way we want to be loved. Please lead us to honor each other as we live together, and help us to settle our differences when conflict invades our home. By your mighty power, allow our personalities to compliment each other. Protect our family from Satan's attacks as we choose to honor and serve you. Amen

Pray for family ministry. We are involved in our local church and community. Because of the many directions our lives take, we pray for God to multiply our time and efforts as we serve:

Holy God, Daily give us the desire to listen to Your voice and be aware of the opportunities that you have given us to join in your work. Lord God, keep us from being a stumbling block to others. By your mighty strength give us courage to stand alone and obey you, even when it is not convenient. We ask that your hand will be on our children.

Even now begin to prepare the person that will be their mate. When the tough times come, give them unprecedented wisdom to make right choices. Show them friends who would challenge and build them up. As they are at school, on the play ground, visiting with friends and going to sports and class, give them protection from evil. And in every situation we ask that for the sake of Your Most Holy Name that they would use their talents and abilities to bring glory and honor to you.

After Roger and I were married, I discovered that his parents and grandparents had prayed for me since Roger was a small child. There is no doubt that my life was changed because of the prayers that were offered in my behalf.

Working as a Family

Colossians 3:23, "Whatever you do, work at it with all your heart, as working for the Lord, not for men."

God ordained work in the Garden of Eden long before he kicked out Adam and Eve. God gave us work as a gift. Remember how satisfied you have felt when you finally complete a project. Do not rob your children of this experience. Allow them the opportunity to feel good about themselves when they have completed a task. They will catch your enthusiasm.

Cleaning day at the Rose house was always an amusing time. Firmly believing that life is what you make it, the goal was to get the work done in a timely manner and enjoy being together while we did it. We started chores, tasks, jobs or whatever you want to call it, while the children were young. They did receive an allowance, but the work they did in our home was accomplished without pay. We used additional chores as a means to obtain extra cash. Making your bed, taking out the trash, cleaning the bathroom, or doing the dishes has always been something that was expected. As the mom, I took them each aside and taught them the proper way to clean a toilet, how to make a bed, clean a bathtub, and mop the floor. Many a day we had more water on the floor than in the tub ... but practice makes perfect. During those times I taught our children that completing a job to the very best of your ability is an act of obedience to God. As we worked we listened to audio music that taught values.

Application:

Teach your children to clean and care for their belongings. Besides establishing the value of an excellent work ethic, they will learn to work together for a common goal and the satisfaction of a job well done. This will serve to their advantage as they grow older and enter school, sports and the work place.

Setting Goals: Family, Ministry, Spiritually

Psalm 119:33–34, "Teach me, O Lord, to follow your decrees, then I will keep them to the end. Give me understanding and I will keep your law and obey it with all my heart."

Once a year we have a goal meeting with each family member. The purpose is to make them aware of the choices they need to make. The beginning of the calendar year or the beginning of the school year is a good time to do this. Roger picks a family verse that we memorize together. The verse becomes our passion or encouragement for the year. We then ask them questions:

- What kind of grades do you want to make this year?
- How will you go about sharing your faith?
- Who will you minister to and how?
- What activities will you be involved in?
- Are you planning your time wisely?
- Are you over committed?
- What talents do you wish to pursue?
- How is your relationship with your sister or brother?
- Are you a good example?
- How can we pray for you?
- Where are you struggling?

This type of dialogue can give you an amazing awareness of where your child might be excelling or struggling. As a parent you are setting the stage for more conversations in the future and giving them purpose for their everyday life. Bear in mind that our objective continues to be one that allows our children to strive toward a goal. Following this meeting have them type up a list of traits or goals that they want to pursue and put them on their bulletin board. You can be their personal cheerleader as they accomplish amazing feats. This is very moving, and also gives you an automatic lead-in to talk about their mismanagement of time or relationships. What an extraordinary opportunity we have to begin to instill in our children personality traits and character that will serve them their entire life. It is a journey you cannot afford to miss.

Follow this example in your relationship to your spouse. It is also important to have goals as a couple. We continually assess our ministry inside and outside of the church. As salt and light, Jesus guides us to be involved *in* the world, but not *of* it. There are many opportunities to serve where your children are already involved. Some of these might be their school, sports and outside activities; you can make a lasting impression by acting as a living example for your children and others around you.

Application:

Coaches all over the globe change their game plan when the rival team is winning. Be ready with a new plan if your old one is not working. Our children learn by example. When we are willing to say that things in our lives need adjustment, they will notice. It just might be the model they need to make a change in their own lives.

Family Prayer Chain

One night a week we would have a family meeting, for us it was Sunday night. We would have a snack, and then our whole family would discuss what the week held in terms of activities, meetings or events. This way we were all on the same page. We knew if Dad had to be out of town, or if someone had a ballgame or perhaps a big test. Since everyone knew we would be meeting, they would come prepared with their prayer request. Everyone was allowed to talk about what he or she was excited about, or maybe not looking forward to, then as a family we would pray. After our prayer time, we would write our request on a paper and pass it to the next person. This list was personal; maybe someone had a request they did not want shared in front of the whole family. That was fine. What a blessing to share our needs with family and know they are being prayed for! This taught our family to pray for one another, and the importance of communicating our needs to each other. On the next meeting night we switched and had a new prayer partner.

This is the special bond I was referring to that is hard work but worth the effort. In the beginning, a family prayer time will not happen naturally. Don't imagine this will be easy or grand every time. Many nights we were grumpy, or weary. Take advantage of these opportunities and benefit from the life lessons that can be taught in difficult circumstances. Consistency shows your children that you want to pray for them and that you are interested in their lives. Commitment to prayer when we are tired and irritable shows them that God is always listening, and that prayer is a discipline that we must learn. Teach by your example how to spend time with God in the weariness of life. It will open their hearts to a new dimension of God's love and faithfulness.

Application:

Assign a name to each person in your family. Make a list of specific prayer needs and give it to the person who will pray for you. Pray for that person, each day for one week, then trade. If your children cannot spell, give them one or two things to remember in their head. Change on the same night every week.

Chapter 3

Kind Deeds

Reflect back to a time when you received an unexpected gift. Remember how it changed the outlook of your whole day? A kind deed is something you do for someone that they do not expect. Kindness is a character trait that God expects us to act out. Kind deeds in your home could be making someone's bed, feeding the dog when it is not your turn, or perhaps putting up a sibling's toy. It might also include setting the table, emptying the trash, or writing an encouraging note.

You are accountable to God for how you live your life and raise your children. Ministry teaches your children kindness and service. Kindness will be a reward in your home life, plus you can teach your children how to cook, clean, and serve others. Parents should teach that kind deeds (ministry) are also used to minister to others outside your home. During the summer months we would get the prayer list from our church on a weekly basis. Each child would pick a shut-in and we would bake homemade treats to take to their home. Our girls learned to serve others, whether the kindness could be returned or not. Ministry is acted out in a visible way and one of the benefits can be a lasting relationship with those you serve. Teach your children to have the character traits that God requires in Galatians 5:22–23. Choices become habits; habits become your character.

Application:

Practice what you want to instruct. Encourage them to make right choices while they are young. "Don't let anyone look down on you because you are young, but set an example for the believers in speech, in life in love, in faith and in purity" (1 Timothy 4:12). Persuade them to put their great ideas to practice. Don't put them off because you are tired or embarrassed. Let them practice the action of love. "Dear children, let us not love with words or tongue but with action and in truth" (1 John 3:18).

Live Out Manners

1 Thessalonians 5:11, "Therefore, encourage one another and build each other up, just as in fact you are doing."

To explain the need for practicing manners we began a mealtime routine of practicing table manners. For instance, we taught our girls to put their napkin in their lap, eat with their mouths closed, and not to eat dessert until all were served and the hostess was seated. We would appoint a leader from one of our children who was the best example of practicing this behavior the day before. If you have boys then you can appoint Sheriff Conduct or Behavior Bouncer. Since our family had all girls they chose Princess Manners and she wore a crown. Let your children help make up a name.

This child was selected after all day good behavior and table manners. The qualifications included, putting your napkin in your lap, not interrupting when someone else is talking, not talking with food in your mouth, chewing with your mouth closed, and if you are a boy, waiting for the women to be seated first. Add other appropriate table manners. The child who is elected to wear the crown or badge is allowed to wear it at each meal for one day. This person does not have to take their plate or help with clean up. At the end of the evening meal, the person with the best manners is elected for the next day. This makes having good manners fun, and as parents you don't have to continually ask them to do certain things.

The funniest thing happened to us. We had a guest over for dinner. The dessert was being served. Our guest was served his pie first. Instead of waiting, our guest began to eat. Our four-year-old daughter promptly slapped his hand and said, "You have to wait for everyone before you can eat!" At least our guest was amused, besides being totally embarrassed. Since that time, we have had the foresight to inform our children that guests do not play Princess Manners. Please be advised that when your children reach the teenage years they will forget their manners. Our hope is that they remember them eventually.

Application:

Teaching manners and respect for family members can encompass all your daily activities. Pray and ask God to show you ways you can implement respect in your own home. Be a daily example as you honor and esteem your own family and other people that cross your path.

Secret code verses

Proverbs 4:27, "Avoid evil, walk straight ahead. Don't take one step off the right path."

Proverbs 12:21, "...no harm befalls the righteous."

Proverbs 13:13, "he who scorns instruction will pay for it."

Sometimes it is necessary to discipline our children when we are in public settings. This is always so awkward and uncomfortable. One morning as I read my Bible I came across a verse that really spoke to me about discipline. It was a simple verse and had a short reference. The Lord gave me the idea that I could sign that verse out with my fingers, or speak the reference only, not the book name. I taught the girls the verse and then explained to them that in the future I would use that reference to warn or correct them. We talked about the importance of immediate obedience and what kind of behavior we expected. I impressed on them what God requires. No one else needed to know what I was saying or expected of them. As a parent, there are times when you need to warn and instruct when their friends are nearby. You can learn to tell them to beware if they are going somewhere when you don't have a chance to talk to them privately. Perhaps if they call you from a friend's house and you need to give instruction, you can gently remind without nagging. They must learn to control their attitudes and actions. You can put a limit on a bad attitude. The Bible does. Ephesians 4:26, "Do not let the sun go down on your anger."

Deal with the problem, and give a solution. Instead of time out, have them memorize a verse. Give them some manual labor. Have them clean a window or be a servant to the offended sibling, (once usually clears up this problem). Serve one another in love. You be the highway patrolman, "Excuse me, you need to sweep the floor. Thank you, have a nice day." Have you ever seen a highway patrolman yelling and screaming like a raving maniac on the side of the road? No. He has the uniform of authority.

Application:

Do you have the uniform of authority, or are you like the policeman who can be bought? If you are the later, then start a new habit. You are the parent, after all. That is the beauty of God's forgiveness. Each day is new and fresh. Consider it a fringe benefit. Get with the program and go iron your uniform. Plan ahead, just in case you run into some lawbreakers. Make a list of on-going chores. Wash the windows, rake the leaves, sweep the porch, wash out the trashcan, and scoop the poop for the pooch. If you really wanted to go crazy you could go to the office supply store and get a receipt pad, then you could really be official. Hand out the punishment on a ticket. It might break the ice of a stressful moment.

Attitude Charts

Deuteronomy 30:19–20, "This day I call heaven and earth as witnesses against you that I have set before you life and death, blessing and curses. Now choose life, so that you and your children may live and that you may love the Lord your God, listen to his voice, and hold fast to him. For the Lord is your life, and he will give you many years in the land he swore to give to your fathers, Abraham, Isaac and Jacob."

Attitudes and actions are typically the source of conflict in the home. Early in our children's lives we began a daily routine of following charts. Charts were made to reflect the kind of attitudes that we wanted to instill in their lives. Give details and make clear to your children the importance of each attitude. It would be wise to start with only four or five things on your chart. Tell them plainly the behavior that you expect. For example:

Treat others the way you want to be treated. Have good manners. Do kind deeds. Be a helper. Say kind things. Share. Obey.

These charts were started before our children could

read, and they were done with incredible consistency. The desired response was to have a home where kindness dwelt. We did not allow unkind words and actions to siblings. (Disclaimer: I did not say there were never any unkind words in our home.) Instead, we chose to build their relationships with kind words and encouragement from each other. Using the charts also gave our children a concrete reminder that we were serious about their behavior without constant nagging. "I urge you to live a life worthy of the calling you have received. Be completely humble and gentle; be patient, bearing with one another in love. Make every effort to keep the unity" (Ephesians 4:1–3).

As a model to your children, there should be no occasion in which you should talk about people. Do not allow hurtful and unnecessary talk in your home. The Bible teaches that we can be sad, happy, joyful, angry, and uncomfortable. But it also teaches self-control. There is no room in our lives for selfishness, smart mouths, or moodiness. Continually teach self-control. We relentlessly prayed that our children would be close to each other and come to depend on one another. In the evening, we put our children to bed by doing their chart, reading a devotional, and singing them songs of Jesus and his love. If there had been a quarrel during the day we could talk about it and teach them how to work it out. At that time, we instructed our children to learn the right response and try it next time. Proverbs 16:20, "Whoever gives heed to instruction prospers, and blessed is he who trusts in the Lord."

At night we would go over each child's chart alone. We would go over the events of the day and ask that child, "Did you do a kind deed? What was it? Did you share?" Maybe that child could not or would not remember. We would prompt them if needed. They received a happy face or star for every completed task. They were given the opportunity to miss four or five per week, and they could not miss three of the same thing in a row. For instance, if they missed "sharing" three times they did not get a prize at the end of the week, (we rarely missed a prize). Then, on Sunday morning when they woke up they received a small treat on their bed. Maybe a pencil, a water toy in the summer, pipe cleaners, a book for worship service. Many times I made their treat something that they already needed: new socks, a hair ribbon, crayons, or colored pencils. It is amazing what a child will do for a sticker.

We can always be ready for the spectacular events that demand our attention, but the annoying circumstances can make us crazy. It is during the mundane that we are caught off guard by the actions of our children. Every day we encounter situations that are hard to handle. When our circumstances become difficult, how do we overcome with victory?

Application:

Remember that every day matters. When we tolerate the difficulty of the time it takes to establish the new attitudes and actions that we want to teach our children, our home life will drastically change. This is profitable for them and also for us. The self-discipline that we teach them will serve them for their whole life. The principle is that you as a parent allow them to choose life, so that they may live.

Bed Time Routine

Deuteronomy 6:6–7, "These commandments that
I give you today are to be upon your hearts. Impress
them on you children. Talk about them when you
sit at home and when you walk along the road,
when you lie down, and when you get up."

Start a new bedtime routine. Let it be a family bond-
ing time. Turn off the television. Get the family to start
gearing down with bath time. Talk about your day as you
bathe them. Depending on their age, read one chapter
of a book, or a short story. You may want to use this as
family devotional time. Turn off the lights and lie down
in bed with them and tell them why you love them. "I
liked how you put up your toys today," "You are a good
example to Sis because you ..." "I love your bright snappy
eyes. They remind me of stars," "I love you as high as the
tallest building."

It has been said that the most important time of the
day is the thirty minutes before you put your children to
bed. When the lights are out, your children will tell you
secrets they won't tell you any other time. Don't miss it.

Use music in their rooms and play Bible verses or
praise music so they will hear God's Word as they go to
sleep. There are so many thoughts that can inspire and
instruct even as they lay in their beds. Repeat the story of
the cross over and over as you put them to bed. Remind
them of what Christ has done for us and that he wants to
come into their hearts and live forever. It sure beats the

heck out of the Three Bears, for heaven's sake! This is the real stuff.

When you share this with your children, tell them, "One day Jesus will come and knock on your hearts door, he will ask if he can come in. You must be thinking about what your answer will be. I certainly hope you say yes." They will ask questions so be ready to answer. Joshua 1:8, "Do not let this book of the law depart from your mouth, meditate on it day and night, so that you may be careful to do everything written in it, then you will be prosperous and successful."

Application:

Do you spend time with God daily? Do your children see you pray? Can they reproduce your life and learn to trust God by your example? Your children want to be a replica of what you live, so make it worth their while. Challenge them to live and love life everyday.

Chapter 4

You are Special

Isaiah 49:16, "See, I have engraved you on the palms of my hands."

We have designed a questionnaire for our children to complete as a communication tool. This practice happens at least twice a year or whenever we notice the quality of our home life shifting or slacking. This is an example that you may want to follow, or you might want to compile your own list of questions. The most important issue is allowing your child to find expression in a non-confrontational manner.

Do we treat you special?

_____

_____

_____

I feel important to you when

_____

_____

_____

What is a way Mom can make you feel special?

_____

_____

_____

What is a way Dad can make you feel special?

_____

_____

_____

Do we show that we are interested in your schoolwork and activities and friends? Is their something we can change or do to act more interested?

_____

_____

_____

Do we have too many rules?

_____

_____

_____

Do you feel loved and accepted for who you are?

_____

_____

_____

It makes me sad when

_____

_____

_____

It makes me glad when

_____

_____

_____

Do you feel like we compare you to others?

_____

_____

_____

It would help me if you would

_____

_____

_____

Do we give you the impression that God is the most important thing to us?

_____

_____

_____

Have we explained to you how important confession of sin is to God?

_____

_____

_____

Do you understand that all sin and disobedience is against God, and that even when you say I am sorry, you must also ask God for forgiveness?

_____

_____

_____

Please pray that I would

_____

_____

_____

Application:

View your child's answers as a glimpse into their hearts. Regard it a privilege to be trusted with their secrets. Do not take personally the feelings that they share. Instead, accept and acknowledge their emotion. Investigate the source of the problem, then do all you can to remedy the basis for their response.

You Are Valuable

1 Samuel 1:27–28, "'I prayed for this child, and the Lord has granted me what I asked of him. So now I give him to the Lord. For his whole life he will be given over to the Lord.'" And he worshiped the Lord there."

One sweet memory we all share is the arrival of our child—whether your child is born in a hospital, at home, or you have adopted from overseas. At some point you may have a christening, or dedication with family or in your church. Many times a special outfit is purchased. When the special day was over I washed and pressed the clothing, then took it to a frame shop and had it placed on a mat board and framed. This was placed on the wall of their room. When they were old enough to understand I would point to the picture and begin to talk about the day they were born. Children want to hear about their value. We began with telling them Genesis 1:27, "So God created man in his own image, in the image of God he created him; male and female he created them." Then we would repeat Genesis 2:7, "The Lord God formed the man from the dust of the ground and breathed into his nostrils the breath of life, and the man became a living being.

The story would go something like this: Remember the verse, "God breathed life into all mankind"? That verse means that we are more valuable than trees, expensive cars or tall buildings simply because God breathed life into us; this also gives us a special union with God. Cars will get old or messed up, trees and buildings will fall down, but we are eternal, we have a soul.

You are precious because of the great price that Jesus paid for you on the cross. When he did this, he was paying the price for all the mistakes that you will ever make. That is how much he loves you. If you were the only person that was ever born he would have died just for you. Even if you live to be ninety-nine, that is a short time compared to eternity. This is one of the reasons why it is important for you to consider asking Jesus to come into your heart and lead and guide you in your life. Jesus wants you to spend your time on earth, as well as all eternity with him.

We were never intended to be self-sufficient. We were never to think just about ourselves. Once we accept Christ, decisions are not ours to make. Because he died he can identify with us. God created us to be filled with the Holy Spirit. The days we separate our self from God we get death because he is our life. He wants us to be a living sacrifice. Some day you might wonder why you are alive. The Bible says we are here to tell others about his great love. John 1:18, "No one has ever seen God, but God the One and Only, who is at the Father's side, has made him known."

Sometimes things happen in our lives that we don't understand, maybe a friend has to move to another city or maybe you don't get to play on the basketball team. Those things can make you wonder if God cares. Remember that he does care and he is always watching over you and wants to help you through difficult times. Since God is the creator of life he can help you find meaning and purpose everyday. You are priceless to God because you are his child. He does not compare you to anyone else. When you feel discouraged and sad remember that God has a plan. You have more value than trees, and the mountains or any other part of nature. God puts more value on your life than all the natural resources on the planet. You can know this is true because God made you in his image and breathed life into you. That makes you very special. You are precious and there is no one else just like you. He always knows where you are and he will never forget you. God made everyone and loves everyone. There is nothing you can do that could make God not love you. Not only that, he loves all the people in the whole world. Never forget that.

Application:

Our children need to know that God does not compare them to their siblings or other children, and the best way they can remember that is for us to tell them over and over. Then of course, it would also help for us not to compare them to other siblings or children.

Bible Verse Name

Psalm 119:105, "Your word is a lamp to my feet and a light to my path."

Use your child's initials to teach them Bible verses. Don't just randomly pick verses. Pray and consider your choices. Select verses that encourage behavior you want to emphasize, or characteristics of God that you want them to remember. For instance, verses that tell about salvation or God's faithfulness, one that informs them of the enemy then another for God's goodness. Here is an example:

E   "Every good and perfect gift is from above, coming down from the Father of the heavenly lights, who does not change like shifting shadows" (James 1:17).

M   "May the words of my mouth and the meditation of my heart be pleasing in your sight O Lord, my rock and my Redeemer" (Psalm 19:14).

I   "I am the vine, you are the branches. If a man remains in me and I in him, he will bear much fruit, apart from me you can do nothing." (John 15:5).

L   "Let us not become weary in doing good, for at the proper time we will reap a harvest if we do not give up" (Galatians 6:9).

Y   "Your enemy the devil prowls around like a roaring lion looking for someone to devour. Resist him, standing firm in the faith" (1 Peter 5:8–9).

A Place of My Own

Your home should be a place where everyone feels safe and secure. Even our children want a place to call their own. The size of your house has nothing to do with the well-being and security they feel. It is the atmosphere and attitude of the family that lives there. As parents we promote unity, sharing and kindness. While it is important to share, it is also essential to have belongings that are just their own. A child should be able to have definite things that they do not have to share and also a certain place to store their "treasures." It can be a drawer, a shoebox in a closet, or a container under the bed. It helps children learn responsibility and trust to know that there are some things that are just their own. Of course we do not want our children storing live animals or food in their special box, however, the items that are special to them may seem worthless to us. Maybe it is the star they made in class, the one with the glitter all over it. Maybe it is a rock they found on the playground that looks like an arrowhead. Let them dream and imagine. But give them a spot that is just their own.

It is amazing to see the difference in attitude and responsibility when a child is given even just a small object or item. In our eyes it may say "wastefulness and foolishness," but in their eyes it says trust and importance.

Application:

Realize that just as you need personal belongings and time alone, so do your children. Give them the attention that they need and the encouragement they desire. Then they will want to be home with you and it will be a secure place. John 14:2–3, "In my Father's house are many rooms; if it were not so, I would have told you. I am going there to prepare a place for you. And if I go and prepare a place for you, I will come back and take you to be with me that you also may be where I am."

Chapter 5

Family Night

Psalm 139:14, "I praise you because I am fearfully and wonderfully made; your works are wonderful, I know that full well."

Family night is an evening that the entire family spends together. Select a night the entire family will be home and do not schedule anything else. This really works best if you can use the same night each week. The special person chooses activities and the dinner menu. The phone is turned off and television is not allowed. When you make this a priority in your week every person feels special. You say to every member in your family, "You are important to me and I want to give you this whole evening." There was a period of about three years when all we ate on family night was hot dogs, fruit salad and chocolate pie. Just remember it is their choice, with in reason. While you plan the menu help your kids learn about the basic food groups.

Activities in our family night included board games, pick-up basketball, bike rides, nature walks, and even croquet. Some of our favorite memories are taking all the books off the shelf and playing library, or store. This was truly a pain. However, it was not dangerous or immoral. It was just a lot of busy work for Mom and Dad. Kids take time and right now, if all they want to do is play with your pots and pans, then drag them out. They will be gone in no time. If you can say yes as often as possible, even though it proves inconvenient for you, then when the time comes to tell them no they will realize there is a good reason.

Board games are real character builders. You play a simple game and everyone wants to win. But only one person can. Do not let your children win. Do not "fix" the game for them. They are not fools. If you let them win you are teaching them it is important to win, and if you can't do it yourself, then Dad will fix it so you can win. This is not a good thing. Better they should learn now that being a good sport is more important than winning, and that cheating dishonors God. Truly, you will be glad when they are thirteen that you did not fix a game for them.

Go on bike rides. At times it took all night just to get around the block, but there are so many lessons in a bike ride. As you ride, say, "Life is like a bike ride. Occasionally you can coast but there are other times when you must pedal hard. Every now and then you see beautiful scenery but occasionally you have to go through rough roads or detours to get to your desired spot. But it is always worth it, and God is always with you. Even being a Christian is like going uphill on a bike. If you stop pedaling you roll backwards. Your walk with God must always be moving or you will lose ground. Sometimes you can't go as fast as others, but keep pushing even when it is hard."

When you walk along the road, be aware of the unusual leaves, funny-shaped rocks, as well as the remarkable shapes of trees. Give each child a small sack to collect treasures. Talk about how God made all these things for us to enjoy and take care of. When you get home, let each child share why they collected each item. Remind them that God made the world for us to enjoy.

Several blocks away from our house there was a church with a big parking lot and two big trees. We started calling it our "secret place." There was certainly nothing spectacular about it, except it had two big trees. We would rest from our ride, take snacks and talk, or try to climb the two trees. If you drove by today you would not notice anything special about this place. However, it was special to us because we decided it was, and because we talked about special things and shared special moments. Discover your own "special place."

Application:

If you cannot spend one night a week together eating a meal and making some memories, creating family unity will be difficult. Unity cannot be built if you are never together. Plan to eat at least one meal a day together. Demand it from your children regardless of their schedules. Encourage each other, talk about your day, and listen with both ears open. Turn off the TV and use meals as an opportunity to find out what your children are learning and what is important to them. Where are they getting information about life? The Bible says it should come from you. Rest assured someone is influencing their choices and thoughts. God clearly states in His Word that you are to equip and inform your children about life. It is your job. God has given you this responsibility because you are capable; do not let this opportunity to shape a life slip through your hands because you feel inadequate. Ask the Lord to give you insight and ideas. He is able.

Summer Months

Use the summer months as a period of exciting spiritual growth for your children. Repeat the story of the cross over and over as you put your children to bed. Remind them of what Christ has done for us, and that he wants to come into their heart and live forever.

Pick a certain day of the week to visit a shut in and take them cookies and treats. Pick a certain day to visit the library and read books all day.

Pick a day to teach your children how to cook and plan meals. All these things can be done while your children are five, six, and seven. When they have learned to read, select themes for them to investigate and learn from the Bible. When you act excited about all the nuggets of truth in the Bible, your children will also be excited to learn for themselves what God says. Galatians 6:9, "Let us not become weary in doing good, for at the proper time we will reap a harvest if we do not give up."

As you clean house, tell your children that God is a God of order, and that our home should be clean and so should our hearts. Give them examples of how they can recognize sin in their lives and how to confess sin so they can have a clean heart. 1 Samuel 16:7, "God does not see the same way people see, people look on the outside of a person, but God looks at the heart."

Pack a picnic lunch, dress those kids up, and take them to eat lunch with their daddy. On the way tell them how terrific their daddy is. Name things that he has done to take care of them and provide for them as well as to keep them safe.

While you rake leaves and plant the garden talk about the earth that God has given us to take care of. When your neighbors are out of town, go and mow their lawn and water their flowers as an act of kindness. Tell them, "We are to love our neighbors as ourselves."

Make a basket of treats to take to a Sunday school teacher or pastor. As you prepare the treats, talk about the fact that God has a plan for every single person. Offer suggestions for them to consider for their own life. What gifts and talents do they possess? What are they curious about? Encourage them to explore thoughts of how they might prepare for the future. "Do you want to be a businessman? A schoolteacher? A dad or mom? Maybe you want to be a preacher so that you can tell others about Christ when you grow up."

Help them to envision the future as you give direction to their dreams. If your children do not have an earthly father or mother do not let that stop you from guiding them to be prepared for the day they accept that responsibility. Declare with steadfast boldness and conviction that they are equal to any task that God has prepared in advance for them to accomplish.

Application:

Encourage your children to discover God's plan through reading the Bible, prayer and family devotions. Give useful ideas of how they can investigate different opportunities to find their own gifts and talents. Let them know that you believe in them and more importantly remind them of God's ever-present desire that they follow him in obedience as they fulfill his purpose for their lives. Regardless of their age it is never to early or too late to speak truth into their lives.

Trip Treats

Romans 12:9–13, "Love must be sincere. Hate what is evil; cling to what is good. Be devoted to one another in brotherly love. Honor one another above yourselves. Never be lacking in zeal, but keep your spiritual fervor, serving the Lord. Be joyful in hope, patient in affliction, faithful in prayer. Share with God's people who are in need. Practice hospitality."

Our family has always been of the attitude that your trip is only as good as the food you bring. As a result, even before we had children, we were in the habit of taking fun snacks everywhere we went. It was established before we got married that we would definitely take vacations. Roger regularly had a fun camping trip or family adventure to recall. I sincerely wanted that for our family. The places we went were not necessarily exotic or outlandish, however they were always refreshing.

As our family grew to three toddlers we realized that to have any kind of enjoyment on a trip we must be organized. Taking ziplock bags, I began to collect index cards, zip-boards, stickers, colors, and anything else that was right for their age. I would save some things back for the trip home or for later in the day. We had candy, (which was a treat) and cheerios, marshmallows, or whatever their favorite snack happened to be. The biggest excitement was the new audio selection. The only requirement was that it must teach values and include Bible verses to learn. We would make a selection and listen to it all across the country, then talk about the values or Bible verses the audio story featured. We had some of the best discussions because they would listen and ask questions and we had the opportunity to respond to a captive audience. Then we talked about how to apply the Scripture to every day life. It has been an important part of their spiritual growth.

Each family member was given a buddy to encourage and take care of on the trip. This is an upbeat way to keep siblings from bickering and squabbling over foolish things. A constructive approach before the trouble begins takes only a little preparation on the parent's part. It is so vital that we maintain an attitude of gratitude in all areas of life.

Parents must set the example by a kind voice and joyful spirit. Be an encourager to your mate. Decide before you get in the car to treat others with kindness. Talk about the stops you will make and the places you will spend the night. Make reservations and stop before you are totally exhausted. I am not so idealistic that I believe no one will ever squabble in the car. However, when those times do occur, confess your sin to God and to each other, and make it right. Then move on. Satan's finest tool is to make us feel unworthy and embarrassed that we act so badly. Yet God forgives. We must also forgive and pick up the pieces; most of the time our pride is the only thing keeping us from sharing a happy moment with the rest of our family. Good grief! Life is just too short for that. What is the point of traveling three hundred miles in total silence? Especially when the foremost crisis is self-ishness? At least that is how it happens in our family.

Everyone cannot always get his or her own way. Someone must be willing to relinquish his or her rights. I would pick the oldest sibling because they should be more mature. These are great times to talk about avoiding the pitfalls of allowing other people to have power over your inner peace. Ask your children, "Who controls your life?" You or your little brother? Should it be the guy at the gas station or the man who pulls in front of you? Maybe even the desk clerk who put you in a smoking room with two twin beds?" It all comes back to my way or God's way. Can we possibly let go of everything, just like our example Jesus Christ? Remember he made him-self nothing, and taking the very nature of a servant, he humbled himself. Jesus gave his life and if we are strug-gling with sharing a coloring book we are in for a life of heartache. This is one of those moments that I do not even want to know what God is thinking. Talk about embarrassing. The bottom line is: we are all accountable to God for how we live our lives, the choices we make, and the fact that all sin is against him. Even in the car on I-20. He expects us to honor and obey. If it isn't taught, it can't be caught.

Use these vacation times to build each other up. Gain knowledge from each other. Take turns and adjust to every situation. When you blow it say, "I'm sorry." Have a great trip and make some memories.

Application:

Vacations are great times to experience "adventure." Regardless of the plans you make you cannot anticipate a traffic jam or a hotel under construction. A flat tire is always a surprise and waiting in line at amusement parks can certainly take the wind out of your sails. Your children and the people around you will be impacted by the attitudes you display in crisis mode. Make it count.

End of Summer Trip

Psalm 127:3–5, "Sons are a heritage from the Lord, children a reward from him. Like arrows in the hands of a warrior are sons born in one's youth. Blessed is the man whose quiver is full of them. They will not be put to shame when they contend with their enemies in the gate."

Before school starts our whole family goes out of town for the weekend. We spend the night in a hotel; we swim and eat out, and buy new clothes for the first day of school. Our family looks forward to this time, and knows it is to prepare for the beginning of school.

Reflecting on our summer, the blessings of God, and the opportunities that will present themselves in the upcoming year are discussed. Somehow the subjects seem less intimidating when you are in a completely different environment. Kids seem to respond better when the conversation is in a casual setting and something else is happening. For instance, buying clothes or swimming.

Remind them that God loves them exactly like they are. Compliment them on an area that has improved. Encourage them to be the very best they can be. This does not necessarily mean A's. Give them ideas for goals that they can attain. If they made all C's last year, then do not insist on A's. Go for the B. Frustration and dissatisfaction can result from asking too much. Go home refreshed and appreciative for what the Lord is going to accomplish this year.

Application:

Despite the fact that new beginnings are fresh and exciting they bring along a certain amount of anxiety as well. Do not expect your children to say they are nervous. Just be ready and use this weekend to remind your children that Jesus came to take away anxiety, fear and uncertainty and he cares for them. Jesus wants to carry their burdens and take away their fear. All they have to do is ask. He will never be too busy or asleep. He is ready to give them the strength and courage they need to start a new year.

Chapter 6

Celebrate Spiritual Birthdays

Acts 4:12, "Salvation is found in no one else, for there is no other name under heaven by which you must be saved."

After your children have accepted Christ as their personal Savior, celebrate on that day every year. Make a special dessert and use candles and sing Jesus loves me. Have your child tell what they remember about that day. When they have said what they want, take the opportunity to tell them ways you have seen them mature. Affirm them as a believer and family member of the great work that Christ has accomplished in their lives. Encourage them to make goals to achieve in this next year. Ask other siblings to join in with positive comments. Talk about the value of being a good sister or brother, and how God demands that we be kind to others and love our family. There is no alternative now that they have surrendered to Christ service. They must honor and obey God. It is a privilege.

It is important that we persuade our children to continually grow in the Lord just as they learn and grow in school. Being a Christian is not effortless; they have a helper with them at all times. Even when we are not there, they have the Holy Spirit. Let them know that the voice inside tells them to be kind and convicts when they disobey. Teach them the importance of confession of sin. Have them memorize 1 John 1:9, "If we confess our sin, then He is faithful and just and will forgive us of our sin and cleanse us from all unrighteousness." Then model that when they say they are sorry. Forgive and forget. Yes, there can be consequences to their sin, but not shame that they do wrong. If you can forgive easily, they will understand God's forgiveness easier.

When we began to celebrate spiritual birthdays, my husband decided he wanted to know the actual day that he asked Christ into his life. We were surprised to discover that Jessica accepted Christ on the same day as her daddy, only twenty-seven years later. We serve a Holy God. Deuteronomy 7:9, "Know therefore that the Lord your God is God. He is a faithful God keeping His covenant of love to a thousand generations of those who love Him and keep His commands."

Application:

By celebrating Spiritual Birthdays you remind your children that growing in the Lord is necessary and that you are paying attention to their spiritual development. Motivate them to work toward a goal. Give spiritual insight, practical advice, and support for whatever situation they are faced with at this time.

Birthday Parties

Psalm 139:13, "For you created my inmost being;
you knit me together in my mother's womb."

Our society offers so many thrilling and alluring opportunities. Many times in the midst of all this, we tend to forget the blessing of our own home and imaginations. Use the resources that you have to plan your birthday parties at home. Besides being cost effective, your children will enjoy the time and effort you spent to prepare this event. Give your child several choices. Here are some ideas to get you started.

The Rodeo

Food:
>   Hot dogs, baked beans and french-fries
>   Serve chuck-wagon style in throw away pie pans

Activities:
- Three-legged race
- Sack race
- Dunk for apples
- Horseshoes

Shaving Cream Party

Everyone wears a swimsuit
Buy several cans of shaving cream, put the kids in the backyard and turn them loose.

The rules:
- No shaving cream in the face
- You may not throw the cans
- You may not squirt shave cream down clothes
- When they have finished, serve watermelon and wash them off with the garden hose.

Miss America Party

Send invitations requesting the girls "dress-up."
When they arrive, let them pick a state.
Print a sash for each girl with the name of her state displayed, and pin on each "contestant."
Play music and have each girl introduce herself.
Make sure that the birthday girl wins the contest!
Eat punch, cookies, and mints.

Surprise Party

Call parents beforehand.
Dress birthday person up in a trench coat and hat.
Go around the neighborhood and pick up the guests.
The birthday person knocks on the door and requests to capture their friend.
Go back to the house and eat breakfast then play a few games.
Let the parents pick up their children at the designated time.

Winter Skating Party

Food:
- Hot cocoa
- Corn dogs
- Cupcakes

Activities:
- Hot potato
- Ice skate

Tear pieces of wax paper in strips (as big as the child's foot).
Give each child two pieces of paper to skate with (take off shoes).
Turn on the music and have them skate the same direction in a circle. Adjust the music to go fast, slow, and then fast again. Change directions.
Have them rest by the fire and read them a story.

MEXICO

Food:
- Eat tacos

Activities:
- Mexican Hat Dance

Divide into teams and make up cheers or skits in Spanish.
Provide instruments for the teams to make up their own music.
Break a piñata.

FRANCE

Food:
- Hot bread, cheese, and fruit

Use candlelight

Activities:
- Recruit other family members to dress up as waiters (with an accent of course) and wear black slacks and white shirts.
- Cut branches off trees to form halos or buy grapevine wreaths.
- Have the girls wrap different colored ribbons around wreaths; let them wear them on their heads as they Tango.
- Prepare fake mustaches for the boys.

CHINA

Food:
- Fried rice and egg rolls

Give them Chinese names as they arrive (ex. Le Chin)
Buy Chinese jump ropes, fans, and umbrellas
Make up dances and bow all the time

Special Occasion Lunches

Proverbs 31:27, "She watches over the affairs of her household and does not eat the bread of idleness."

Special lunches at school make your child feel special. This tradition started out innocently enough on Valentine's Day. No matter what grade or which child, I soon realized that they were not going to get the right Valentine from the right classmate. Therefore, to offset the disappointment I started making special Valentine lunches. We had heart sandwiches with heart cookies and red strawberry pop. All these things were tied up with red ribbons in a decorated sack, which had the proper greeting on the outside. To complete the lunch I made a special note with a Scripture and word of encouragement.

Somewhere down the road it got out of hand and I began to do Easter lunches with bunnies, or Christmas lunches with the Christmas story. When going on field trips to the zoo I would make a special Zoo Lunch. It would have animal crackers, and a pop wrapped in Reynolds wrap with pipe cleaner ears to make it look like an animal. I would also draw a face with magic markers. You can find all types of theme napkins and stickers. Put your child's name on the outside of the sack, name the event, and add something that goes along with the event inside. A little unexpected surprise reminds them that you are remembering them on this day.

Application:

Have you been on a field trip lately? Somehow this is the time that all the unruly children dare others to take part in mischief and wrongdoing. Before the event, remind your child to live in obedience and make right choices. Put a note in their lunch that reminds them that Jesus has set the example that we must follow. Remember, the difference between extraordinary and ordinary is that you do a little "extra." Use every occasion to inspire and give practical insight.

Easter Celebration

The Easter bunny comes to our house on the Saturday before Easter; while Sunday is saved for remembrance of the resurrection of Jesus Christ. 2 Corinthians 5:21, "God made him who had no sin to be sin for us, so that in him we might become the righteousness of God."

When the neighbors pull out their fluffy bunnies, I add my Easter egg basket to the table and allow the children to play with it all season. The use of visual aids can be very thought provoking. Make a basket of eggs that contain the events surrounding Christ's crucifixion. Before our Easter lunch we each take turns opening the eggs and describing the contents. Each numbered egg also has a verse of Scripture that describes the reason for the item. If you have small children, it is a wonderful tool to use throughout the year. Use a small basket and fill it with numbered eggs. Set them on the fireplace or a shelf in your family room. Allow your children to open the eggs at anytime, providing they put them up when they are finished. This will give you the opportunity to talk about the sequence of events that led to Christ's death. When they ask questions you will be prepared with verses in hand. Some questions they might ask could be: Did it hurt Jesus when they tied his hands? Was the cross heavy? Why did they want to hurt him?

This will also give you the opportunity to tell them that we all make mistakes. None of us is perfect. That is why Christ came and died for our sin. Jesus took our place, our punishment. Tell the story again, One day he will knock at their heart's door, and the choice they must make to ask him into their heart.

1. Dime   Matthew 26:14–16

2. Cracker   Luke 22:19

3. Rope   John 18:12

4. Robe   Matthew 27:28

5. Crown   Matthew 27:29

6. Cross   John 19:17

7. Nail   Mark 15:24

8. Sponge   John 19:28–30

9. Spear   John 19:34

10. Gauze   John 20:6–8

11. Rock   Luke 24:2

12. Empty   Mark 16:6–7

Application:

To receive Christ as Lord and Savior is the single most important decision anyone will ever make. With strong conviction and tenderness explain why Easter has changed the outcome of sin and death. Boldly proclaim the significance of Christ's death on the Cross, the Resurrection, and the power of the blood that was shed on the Cross. Ask God to give you practical ideas to provide the details they need to understand his love and sacrifice.

Sundays are Special Days

Exodus 20:8, "Remember the Sabbath day and keep it holy."

Mark 2:27–28, "Then he said to them, 'The Sabbath was made for man, not man for the Sabbath. So the Son of Man is Lord even on the Sabbath.'"

We began preparation for Sunday on Saturday night. We laid out everyone's clothes, including that missing sock that you could never find. We called it playing Flat man. Hair bows, slips, and shoes and socks were all accounted for at this time. We gave the girls two outfits to choose from, and no one was ever allowed to change their mind the next morning. We didn't need the diversion of changing clothes several times. If we were out late we did not let that keep us from attending church. We get up early for school, band, sports, garage sales, and work. Will we offer God less? Teach your children by example, that Sunday is a gift from God. This is the day God intended for us to use as a spiritual, mental, and physical refreshing of our lives. If we do not get up and go to church with a happy attitude, we teach our children that other things are more important than worship.

On your way to church talk about what good things will happen. During the trip home talk about what you learned and how you can apply it to your life. If your little boy loves his Sunday school teacher, the one that drives you crazy, then be appreciative that he likes to go to church. Don't be jealous and tell your kid what a jerk he is in the business world. Keep your lips locked and be relieved that Jesus doesn't have favorites and that he likes you even though you are judgmental. Take advantage of the fact that while your children are small they must go where you lead. Enjoy fellowship at church and benefit from what it offers. Then when your children get their driver's license they will gladly come to worship.

Has it ever occurred to you that Satan has a few pals at church too? Stay clear of them and don't let them lead you into sin. Don't let others spoil your worship. Genesis 4:6, "Why is your face downcast? If you do what is right, will you not be accepted? But if you do not do what is right, sin is crouching at the door; it desires to have you, but you must master it."

Application:

Sometimes, sin crouches at the door of our house or at the entrance of our church. Lurking. Waiting. Doing everything in its power to destroy our worship. Let's all be well grounded in our faith and keep our eyes open, our mouths shut, and our hearts clean. If we want our children to be present at church then we must enjoy and benefit from it as well. Do not drop them off at the door and head back home. Go with them. When we wait for a crisis to arise before we call on God, our actions show that God is only for emergencies, not everyday.

Chapter 7

The Talk

During the sixth grade, or before middle school, arrange a time to talk with your child about sex. If you have boys, the responsibility goes to the man. Decide beforehand what to share. You can do this on the weekend, during the day, or in the evening. You might even check them out of school for the day and shop, or go to lunch but the main purpose is to talk. Several days before, I would tell my daughter what we were going to do, and she would be able to ask me any question. This gives them time to get used to the idea, and also to look forward to the event. "It is God's will that you should be sanctified: that you should avoid sexual immorality; that each of you should learn to control his own body in a way that is holy and honorable, not in passionate lust like the heathen, who do not know God" (1 Thessalonians 4:3–5).

On this day, nothing is off limits. Tell them that sex is God's gift to married people; it is fun, and a blessing. Talk about purity, God's plan for their future, and other relevant subjects. It is unfortunate that these issues have to be discussed at such an early age. However, everyone else is talking about it. For that reason you want to make sure they get accurate facts. You do not want you children to be confused and bewildered because you feel self-conscious about the subject matter. There may not be a lot of feedback, but just keep talking. How your child accepts the information is irrelevant to the significance of relaying the facts. This is your chance to speak truth into their lives as you encourage them to be sexually pure. The foundation is laid because you introduced the subject; this takes the pressure off your child and gives them courage to ask questions at another time.

Lunch should be at a nice quiet restaurant. At this time talk about God's plan for them and the way they should conduct themselves. Proverbs 7:7–23 is a wonderful passage for what girls or boys should never become. These verses address actions, looks, dress and behavior. Use 1 Thessalonians 4:3–6 and 1 Corinthians 6:19–20. Entreat them to make a commitment to God to stay pure until marriage. Encourage them to sign a covenant of purity; you may even present them with a purity ring. Be sensitive to your child. If they do not want to make a commitment or they want to think about it then you must let them. Remember that this is their decision; you can only make them aware of their options. I acknowledge that you cannot cover all things in one day. Still, this is a great way to get started. As they get older there are many more issues to discuss. For instance, dating, meeting the opposite sex at the mall, holding hands, and kissing.

Application:

Our family learned early on that before they went anywhere with a guy, he would be interviewed by Dad. This rule has been a lifesaver more than once. Many spur of the moment dates have been thwarted because of this rule. Never once have I been sorry that we made it. When your daughter knows there will be an interview before a date she is really a lot more selective with her choices. If you have sons, give them specific examples of how to treat a girl. Show them Biblical facts and examples of the trouble boys and men faced because they lacked self-control (Sampson, David, Amnon). When your son comes home from his date ask questions and hold him accountable to wholesomeness and purity.

Quality Time with Dad

> Ephesians 6:4, "Fathers, do not exasperate your children; instead, bring them up in the training and instruction of the Lord."

My husband is very purpose driven. From the time our children were born, the Lord laid it on his heart to teach them proper behavior with the opposite sex. Because of this, Roger would take them to lunch individually. During these times he would open their doors, compliment them on their behavior and thank them for the opportunity to spend time with them. The older they got, the more in-depth the conversation became. This gave them all special time with their dad, but it also taught them that they were important to him. We have discovered that the one-on-one time makes a huge difference in their response and attitude. This routine can be adapted to almost any schedule. Our routine changes from year to year, depending on the school location and other commitments. Many years he took them to lunch or breakfast. Other times he took them for an ice cream in the evening. When and where is not important. The time involvement and the message it sends is the issue. Our children need to know that we care. If we do not take time to teach them how to act, then who will? Some people say they don't get much quantity time with their children, but they make up for it with quality. It seems to me in Deuteronomy when it talks about walking in the road, rising up, lying down and sitting at home, and all that stuff, that God is saying, "Dear parents, spend quality and quantity times with your children."

Boys need to have special times with their dad also. If there is a hobby or sport you both enjoy, you can use that time to build your relationship. Showing your child they are important is the objective. Your responsibilities and obligations are the same. As with daughters, the boys just need to know that they are valuable too. They will learn more from the way you treat your wife, and what you say about her.

Date your Mate

Matthew 19:5–6, "'For this reason a man will leave his father and mother and be united to his wife, and the two will become one flesh?' So they are no longer two, but one. Therefore what God has joined together, let man not separate."

From the time our children begin to walk, we are supposed to be working ourselves out of a job. After our children have come and gone, our mates will still be with us. As a couple, you will never survive if you don't spend time with one another. You must work at maintaining that relationship. We give so much energy to our children and friends. Is there anything left for the one we love? Make it a point to show your children that your spouse is the most important person in the family. Send your mate cards or flowers; just be sure to treat them special. Make a date to go out to lunch once a week. If your children are in school this will work as a free baby sitter. Sometimes I pack a picnic lunch. On special occasions like birthdays or anniversaries, do something out of the ordinary. My husband's office is thirty miles away. However, on our anniversary I drove downtown, found his suburban on the sixth floor of the parking garage and shoe polished the windows. I wrote: "Happy Anniversary. You are the best husband in the whole world. I love you." Send your husband fun packages at work. Everybody loves to get mail. I have sent my husband his favorite snack food, pictures of when we were dating, and even a new shirt. Use your imagination. Kidnap your spouse from work and take them away for the weekend.

Since God's plan is unity in our homes and family, husbands and wives should be in agreement in the plan and purpose of home life as well. The biggest hindrance is demanding your own way, universally known as selfishness. You must be willing to yield if you want unity. Our home will only be as strong as our relationship with our spouse. As you take those special lunches and weekend dates express what a blessing your mate is to you.

Application:

Work and plan together to develop inward qualities that will benefit your relationship and family. Recognize and acknowledge areas of your relationship that need to be stretched or reeled in. Be wary of conflicts that arise from attitudes, actions and situations and brainstorm together as you determine ways to avoid those pitfalls in home and family life.

Chapter 8

Will over Emotion

Galatians 2:20, "I have been crucified with Christ, and I no longer live, but Christ lives in me. The life I live in the body, I live by faith in the Son of God."

In the heart of each mother lies the aspiration to create a home filled with harmony. That desire can only come to pass by using the guidelines that Christ has set before us. Jesus has called us to live a life of sacrifice. More often than not, peace can be attained in your home by merely putting away self. The Bible tells us to be dead to ourselves and alive to Christ. Galatians 5:22–23, "But the fruit of the Spirit is love, joy, peace, patience, kindness, goodness, faithfulness, gentleness and self-control. Against such things there is no law."

Have you realized as the mom your actions and attitudes either build up, or destroy the tone of your home? The joy in your actions and attitudes has an astonishing effect on the other members of the family. Ponder just this morning, or even last night. What result did you have on your family? Attitude is so powerful that even if a word is never spoken the ambiance tells all. There are days that I am pretty happy about that, however, more times than not, the pressure of that responsibility can be overwhelming. Jesus has called us to be dead to ourselves, and alive to Christ. Dead to discord, jealousy, fits of rage, selfish ambition and hatred. Imagine this. You attend a funeral and the vocalist is singing. Suddenly the corpse jumps from the casket and says, "That is not what I wanted you to sing, and I hate these flowers, and why is he a pallbearer?" Absurd. Yet, in the same manner, Christ calls us to a life of being dead to ourselves. Dead to selfishness, bitterness, anger. He wants to take all those contrary emotions and replace them with positive traits. These characteristics are not something we can attain on our own strength. "God has poured out His love into our hearts by the Holy Spirit, whom he has given us" (Romans 5:5). Christ wants to work in us and through us to produce these qualities. Keep in mind that God's commands are not directed towards our emotions, but to our wills.

Cooperate with God as he develops your inward qualities. Focus on more of him and less of you.

When I accepted Christ, I was forgiven immediately but I had eighteen years of bad habits to overcome. The third chapter of Colossians became my theme song, to set my mind on things above. More than anything I wanted to forget the lies I had been told of being worthless, and I wanted to stop being a victim. Even though this was my target, many of my days were spent being discouraged because to be a new creation seemed like too big of a job. After about six months of losing the battle in my mind I was given some helpful advice. "Take it one day at a time." Do not worry about tomorrow. For only today, work at being a new creation. Remain steady, not happy or sad, just constant. I was all over the map with my emotions and I had no discipline. Then I realized that you do it one day at a time until it becomes a habit. My friend encouraged me to get up thirty minutes early because once the day starts it is harder to find thirty minutes. So I did. I read a Psalm and one proverb and one chapter out of the New Testament. I started trying to do it two days in a row then three and so on. It actually made a big difference in my life to be in control of something, but it also made a big difference to have a week go by and know that I had disciplined myself. Gradually I began to be more confident. The Word of God changed me. One of the most desperate feelings I have ever had is just the sense that I was not adequate. That no matter what I did I could not measure up to anyone's expectations. By just having a daily quiet time the Word of God restored me daily, and as I lived daily, the ocean of despair shrank.

Anger and ridicule had left me insecure and afraid. Yet, when I realized by faith, how much God loved me and that I was a special creation, I wanted everything he had for me. We have such a powerful God. Whether I realized it or not, the Lord was in the process of making me surrender, that I might conform to his image. His eye is on eternity while my focus was on myself. Every day he plans to release the fragrance of his power through us.

In order for this to happen we must walk with him daily. As we build ourselves up in God's Word we become prepared for the random events that come everyday.

I must tell you that you cannot expect to be a bundle of joy in one short weekend. However, God is true. The Psalms say over and over, "I will exalt you my God, I will praise you, and I will bless you." Never once in the Psalms does it say I feel like praising Jesus today. You just do it. It is an act of obedience and a sacrifice of praise. Yes, it can be a sacrifice. The more you praise him out of practice, the more your heart desires to praise him. Remember, choices become habits and habits become your character. Choose praise.

The world says, "If it feels good, do it." We buy into that. We don't want to do what is painful, stressful or boring. So we miss God's blessing. We say, "Well that makes me a hypocrite if I do something I don't mean." But this is not true. If you have accepted Christ as Savior you can be dead to yourself and alive to him. Disobedience is what makes you a hypocrite. Do you imagine Jesus felt like walking across the water in the storm or being tempted by Satan and going hungry forty days? Please remember that he was also beaten and betrayed by his friends then hung to die on a cross. Would you call him a hypocrite because he said, "Let this cup pass from me?" I think not. Why did he do it? Obedience. Will over emotion. He knew that there was something *better* waiting for him. It is the same for us. Jesus knew we would need help, and he knew it would be hard. That is what the Holy Spirit is all about and that is why Paul said, "I beat my body and make it my slave" (1 Corinthians 9:27).

Application:

I am not saying you can never have emotion. Go on living, but continue to pursue Christ likeness and be aware of the prompting of the Holy Spirit. Let him guide you into truth and righteousness daily. Spend time with him. Pray. Ask God for guidance when you face conflict. Our family strives for an "even" level of emotion when we face trials or triumph. We strive for the middle, not the top or bottom of the mountain. At least it gives you a place to begin. Your character can only be changed by the power of the Holy Spirit. No amount of discipline can continually be successful. 2 Timothy 1:7, "God did not give us a spirit of timidity, but a spirit of power, of love and of self-discipline." We must have the self-discipline to ask for his power and love to flow through our lives, our homes, and our families. This ought to start with the parents.

The Gift of the Holy Spirit

Hebrews 7:25, "Therefore he is able to save completely those who come to God through him, because he always lives to intercede for them."

Our children learned this verse off of a children's audiotape. We talked about the verse and what it meant. However, on occasion putting the verse to use totally changes how you feel about it. Our family had moved to a new town. This of course meant a new church and new friends and youth group. The time came for our girls to go on a mission trip with the new youth group. Jessica was a ninth grader and Sarah was a seventh grader. We were all pretty apprehensive about the trip. Even though we loved our church, the sponsors, and youth, the thought of sending them off for eight days with these people was a little unnerving. I reminded the girls that if they ever needed anything they could ask a sponsor. Once more we expressed our love to them and gave them the phone card. We shared Hebrews 7:25, reminding them the Holy Spirit is always with them. For instance, maybe you cannot use a phone, or you don't want to share your need with another person. Remember that Jesus is always with you and if you need us to pray for you then tell the Lord. He will prompt us with his Holy Spirit.

One night I woke up suddenly. It was four o'clock in the morning. I felt an urgent need to pray for Sarah. As we prayed for both our girls we began to feel some sense of relief. The next morning Sarah called us from Santa Fe. She told us this story.

They had been staying in a hotel. Sarah was exhausted from their busy schedule. That night, in her weary state she walked right out of her hotel room. The door locked behind her. When she realized what had happened, she was in the hallway. She knew everyone on the floor was in her group, but she could not get anyone to wake up. She knocked and knocked on doors. She was tired and terrified. Finally she realized that she would have to go downstairs and outside to get to the front desk. She ran as fast as she could. However, the desk clerk was not impressed with her story. (Why would a thirteen year old be in the lobby in the middle of the night)? He would not give her a room key until he talked to someone in her room. When they called her room, her friend answered the phone and promptly went back to sleep. Of course she dropped the phone on the floor first.

At last the desk clerk gave Sarah a key. She went back to her room and cried. She told us of her fear and that she had seen a man outside, so she was very afraid to go to the lobby. Finally she realized it was her only choice and she made it back safely to her room. When I asked her what time it was, she said, 3:00 in the morning. That is exactly the same time it is in Oklahoma with the time-zone change. When I told her that we had both been awake the whole time praying for her, she was astonished. What a blessing to see God's hand in her life. Who knows what evil was lurking that God protected her from that night. No one in our youth group will ever forget that story.

Application:

Remind your children that God is the source of all the power in the universe and that He is always ready and available to meet their need. All they have to do is ask. Teach them how to depend on the Holy Spirit. He desires to show his power because nothing is impossible with God. Don't leave life to chance! Pray and ask God to stand in the gap for you and your children.

Endure Life's Struggles

As believers in Jesus, we are in a battle that we must take seriously. We must fight for the unity of our home and family. We must be forever true to the cause of Jesus Christ, and never desert our standard. "Endure hardship with us like a good soldier of Christ Jesus. No one serving as a soldier gets involved in civilian affairs-he wants to please his commanding officer" (2 Timothy 2:3–4).

Instruct your children that as followers of Jesus we must not look, act, or cooperate with the enemy. Remind them that if everyone else is "doing it" then maybe that is the best reason they should not. Use a theme to teach them preparation for life in the home and church. Some examples might be a soldier, an athlete, or a gardener.

How does a Soldiers Defend?

- Obey their leaders.
- Endure in good and bad times
- Work together for the cause
- Keep their weapons with them at all times.
- Be prepared for surprise attacks.
- Do not willingly walk in to enemy grounds.

Verses to inspire Soldiers:
- Do not fight among yourselves.
    2 Timothy 2:24
- Cooperate and encourage
    Numbers 32:6–7
- Communicate
    Colossians 4:6, Ephesians 4:29
- Keep your head in all situations
    2 Timothy 4:5
- Endure hardship
    2 Timothy 2:3–4
- Be strong
    1 Corinthians 15:58, Daniel 6:16

How does an Athlete Play?

- Obey the rules.
- Listen to their coach.
- Keep their focus in the game.
- Be willing to change their strategy in order to win the game.
- Have self-discipline, eat a proper diet, have proper exercise.
- Don't look back or you lose your lead.
- Stay in the race.

Verses to inspire Athletes:
- Run to win
    1 Corinthians 9:24–27
- Keep your focus
    2 Corinthians 4:17–18
- Press on
    Philippians 3:12–14
- Physically fit
    Hebrews 12:1
- Resist discouragement
    Galatians 5:7–8

How can a Gardener produce?

- Prepare the earth
- Plant the seed

- Care for their crops
- Work in season and out

Verses to inspire Gardeners:
- Recruit help
  Matthew 9:37
- Plant and Life cycle
  1 Corinthians 15:36–39
- Reap what you sow
  2 Corinthians 9:6–10
- Persevere
  Galatians 6:9
- Endure
  Hebrews 12:11
- Enjoy the harvest
  2 Timothy 2:6

Explain the message of John 10:10, "The thief comes only to steal and kill and destroy: I have come that they may have life, and have it to the full." While we teach them that God has a plan for their lives, it would be reasonable to inform them that the devil also has a plan. In fact, he will stop at nothing to tear them down. He uses actions, attitudes, and situations. We must seek continual protection from his lies. This can only be accomplished by spending time in the truths of God's Word. If we do not keep in touch with with him everyday, we will miss out on the battle plan. The devil uses selfishness, anger, apathy, weariness, jealously, and busyness to keep us from what is really important.

The pressures of raising a family in a lost world are overwhelming. We cannot do it alone. We must rely on God for power and insight. The only "normal" that you can count on is that your home life will constantly change as your children grow, mature, and face unpredictable changes. God's Word is the only constant source of strength and power. Allow his presence to rule in your home. When the struggles and battles come, remember, his power is made perfect in weakness. Then rely on his power to get you through. John 16:33, "I have told you these things' so that in me you may have peace. In this world you will have trouble. But take heart! I have overcome the world."

You have the privilege of shaping your child's future. Make it count. Treasure each day. Don't be so caught up in the busyness of life that you miss living. Make new memories and cherish old ones. Use the gifts that God has given you to make your family life special and unique. When you encounter situations that you do not know how to handle, go to God's Word. There is no situation in this world that has not been dealt with. James 1:5, "If any of you lacks wisdom, he should ask God, who gives generously to all without finding fault, and it will be given to him."

Application:

Fear and frustration are obstacles that keep us from trusting in God's power, but more importantly they cultivate discouragement. We know fear and frustration are not from God. Then where is it from? The enemy! Since we will always be exposed to the opinions of the world, to temptation and deceit, we must also remember that the pressures of this world will not suddenly vanish. We must enter God's rest instead of trying to fix everything our self. Strength and courage are developed during testing times. Suffering for doing the will of God is part of our heritage. Hard times can either make us spiritually powerful or destroy our faith. These are life lessons! Now is a good time to teach our children to learn how to master fear and endure life's struggles.

Chapter 9

Lunch Notes

When our children were young I started putting a little note in their lunches. If I forgot they were quick to let me know that they missed it. It was clear that I had to get a better plan because it took quite a bit of time to get three notes written. I began to mass-produce verses and notes at my own pace. Many times I created them a month at a time. Sometimes I did a series, for instance the ABC's, or self-control, faith, love, or any other topic. God honors our effort when our goal is to bring him glory. When I recount the times that those verses ministered to our children and their friends, I am thankful that I took the time. What started as a quick gesture of support became a topic of interest for our family. The notes prompted several conversations at school and opened opportunities to encourage classmates as well. This was the talk of the lunch table. Interest mounted as the note was read out loud. Several times a friend insisted on keeping the note. When our children are bombarded at school with bad language, bad attitudes, and coarse remarks, a Bible verse can make all the difference. I was convicted to put a Scripture they could pray or be encouraged by. In the pages that follow I have included several pages of lunch notes that you can copy and put in your children's lunches.

Stand Firm

You must be armed for battle you must not fight alone. God goes before you. He will protect his own. Exodus 14:13–14, "Do not be afraid. Stand firm and you will see the deliverance the Lord will bring you today. The Lord will fight for you; you need only be still."

Regardless of how crazy this world may seem to be, God is in control of all. He cares for you and me. Psalm 33:11, "The plans of the Lord stand firm forever, the purpose of his heart through all generations."

When I make mistakes it is a relief to know that Jesus can fix my mess ups no matter where I go. Psalm 37:23–24, "If the Lord delights in a man's way, he makes his steps firm; though he stumble, he will not fall, for the Lord upholds him with his hand."

You can change your address, attitude, and even your hair. But nothing will change the fact that God will always care. Psalm 89:2, "I will declare that your love stands firm forever, that you established your faithfulness in heaven itself."

Get ready. You are going to be tested! Stand firm in your faith, even if you're arrested. Matthew 24:13, "He who stands firm to the end will be saved."

It is simple to be committed to God when no one is around. The test will come as a surprise…don't get shoved into the ground. 1 Corinthians 10:12, "So, if you are standing firm, be careful that you don't fall!"

There are new battles to face everyday. Prepare. Pray. Plan. Trust in God. His power will make you stand. 1 Corinthians 15:58, "Therefore, my dear brothers, stand firm. Let nothing move you. Always give yourself fully to the work of the Lord, because you know that your labor in the Lord is not in vain."

Honor the commitment that you made to God by not giving in to your feelings. 1 Corinthians 16:13–14, "Be on your guard; stand firm in the faith; be men of courage; be strong. Do everything in love."

God's love for you is tested, tried and true. 2 Corinthians 1:21, "Now it is God who makes both us and you stand firm in Christ."

Never under estimate the freedom you feel when you ask God to forgive you of your sin. It will weigh you down; don't keep carrying it around. Maybe every time you take a shower, you can call on his forgiveness and power. Galatians 5:1, "It is for freedom that Christ has set us free. Stand firm, then, and do not let yourselves be burdened again by a yoke of slavery."

Christians must stand together if we are going to win the battle. Do you have a Christian friend? Philippians 1:27, "Whatever happens, conduct yourselves in a manner worthy of the gospel of Christ."

Have you ever been in a storm of grief and despair? God is your anchor. He is always there. Hebrews 6:19, "We have this hope as an anchor for the soul, firm and secure."

Do not try to go to battle all alone. Remember Jesus is strong when we are weak. His power is unleashed when we call on his Holy name. 1 Peter 5:8–9, "Be self-controlled and alert. Your enemy the devil prowls around like a roaring lion looking for someone to devour. Resist him, standing firm in the faith, because you know that your brothers throughout the world are undergoing the same kind of suffering."

Grace

Grace, mercy, forgiveness and pardon, gifts from Jesus as sweet as a garden. John 1:14, "The Word became flesh and made his dwelling among us. We have seen his glory, the glory of the One and Only, who came from the Father, full of grace and truth."

Don't let your knowledge support you; trust what God knows. Let him do it for you. Proverbs 3:34, "He mocks proud mockers, but gives grace to the humble."

Lose by omission, lose by default, and relinquish the peace you could have in your heart. Whatever you hold that takes your peace, throw it down, experience release.

Luke 12:15, "Then he said to them, 'Watch out! Be on your guard against all kinds of greed; a man's life does not consist in the abundance of his possessions.'"

Jesus loves you it is true. By his grace he took your place so that your sin could be erased; ask him into your heart, be born again. John 1:16, "From the fullness of his grace we have all received one blessing after another."

When you do something wrong, ask to be forgiven. The law was abolished when Jesus' life was given. Romans 6:14, "For sin shall not be your master, because you are not under law, but under grace."

When you are tired and weary, troubled and sad, rely on God like he is all you have. That is what he wants, that is what he is for, to double your strength, when you need some more. 2 Corinthians 9:8, "And God is able to make all grace abound to you, so that in all things at all times, having all that you need, you will abound in every good work."

Life is a battleground for Christians like you. Fix your eyes on Jesus and he will see you through. 2 Corinthians 12:9, "My grace is sufficient for you, for my power is made perfect in weakness."

I look at you and I am proud to see, a child who is dear to me. Thanks for the choices you have made and for the life you lead. I am thankful for your stand for God and your commitment to do His will. 2 Corinthians 13:14, "May the grace of the Lord Jesus Christ, and the love of God, and the fellowship of the Holy Spirit be with you all."

It was bought with a price, but is free for the taking. God gave us grace when he died in our place. Ephesians 2:8–9, "For it is by faith you have been saved, through faith-and this is not from yourselves; it is the gift of God not by works, so that no one can boast."

If you don't have something kind to say don't say anything at all. Colossians 4:6, "Let your conversation be always full of grace, seasoned with salt, so that you may know how to answer everyone."

Do you feel a little weary? One more disappointment and you won't be able to take it? God did not ask you to live a perfect life. Jesus asked you to give him your life. Allow him to be your control management! James 4:6, "He gives us more grace, that is why the Scripture says, God opposes the proud but gives grace to the humble."

Serve

When the day is hot, when your day turns bad, remember the troubles that Shadrach, Meshach, and Abednego had. They realized what it meant to serve God, even when it hurt. They were willing to give their lives for the cause of Christ; they did not even expect him to save them from the fire. Daniel 3:16–18, "O Nebuchadnezzar, we do not need to defend ourselves before you in this manner. If we are thrown into the blazing furnace, the God we serve is able to save us from it, and he will rescue us from your hand, O king, But even if he does not, we want you to know, O King, that we will not serve your gods or worship the image of gold you have set up."

Satan's plan is to lead you away from the glory and honor of serving Christ today. Wherever you go, whatever you do, Satan will seem to offer a better plan for you—but inside your heart you will see, Christ is saying, "Pick him, or me." Galatians 6:7–8, "Do not be deceived: God cannot be mocked. A man reaps what he sows. The one who sows to please his sinful nature from that nature will reap destruction; the one who sows to please the Spirit, from the Spirit will reap eternal life."

Your mission today is for others to see that God will use anyone, you or me ... his grace is the distinction in your life and mine. Share his grace with others and have a pleasant time. Philippians 1:4–6, "I always pray with joy because of your partnership in the gospel from the first day until now, being confident of this, that he who began a good work in you will carry it on to completion until the day of Christ Jesus."

This is a hard task God has set before you: to serve him day and night. It can be done with strength from above; take a moment and bask in his love. Matthew 11:28–30, "Come to me, all you who are weary and burdened, and I will give you rest. Take my yoke upon you and learn from me, for I am gentle and humble in heart, and you will find rest for your souls. "For my yoke is easy and my burden is light."

Whenever younger people are around, model how a servant of God should look, act, and sound. They really may not know; in you they should see precisely what God would want them to be. Titus 2:7–8, "In everything set them an example by doing what is good. In your teaching show integrity, seriousness and soundness of speech that cannot be condemned, so that those who oppose you may be ashamed because they have nothing bad to say about us."

What Christ wants from you is obedience—your heart. God can do much through you. You just have to be a willing subject. Don't try to do life all on your own. John 14:21, "Whoever has my commands and obeys them, he is the one who loves me. He who loves me will be loved by my Father, and I too will love him and show myself to him."

I am so thankful for your encouragement to others. There are so many occasions to be a helper this week; I know I can count on you. My heart is filled with delight as I think of you and your relationship to our Savior. Philemon 1: 4–5, "I always thank my God as I remember you in my prayers, because I hear about your faith in the Lord Jesus and your love for all the saints."

Worry

Remember, Jesus was up before you were, and he knows what this day holds. Just trust. Matthew 6:25, "Therefore I tell you, do not worry about your life, what you will eat or drink; or about your body, what you will wear."

You read the Bible everyday, confess your sin when you pray. When those hard times come your way, trust the Lord, he will tell you what to say. Matthew 10:19, "But when they arrest you, do not worry about what to say or how to say it. At that time you will be given what to say."

You must remember as you scurry through life that you can do more with God in one hour than you can in a lifetime without him. Matthew 6:27, "Who of you by worrying can add a single hour to his life?"

Humility is when we leave everything up to God. Allow God to be in control of your day, and then see what a great job he can do. 1 Peter 5:7, "Cast all your anxiety on him because he cares for you."

Don't insist that life has to run according to your own timetable. Consider others and adjust when necessary. 1 Peter 4:7, "Do not be anxious about anything, but in everything, by prayer and petition, with thanksgiving, present your request to God."

Comfort

You are God's masterpiece. He created you. That gives your life significance. Genesis 1:27, "So God created man in his own image, in the image of God he created him; male and female he created them."

God looks on your life with compassion and grace. Be sure to treat others just like he treats you. John 15:12–13, "My command is this: Love each other as I have loved you. Greater love has no one than this, that he lay down his life for his friends."

Fulfilling God's purpose will be your life's greatest accomplishment. Ephesians 2:10, "For we are God's workmanship, created in Christ Jesus to do good works, which God prepared in advance for us to do."

God deals with each one of us on an individual basis. He is the one we need to please. Galatians 1:10, "Am I now trying to win the approval of men, or of God? Or am I trying to please men? If I were still trying to please men, I would not be a servant of Christ."

God has a specific task for each one of us. There is an actual blueprint that Christ has for you to follow. Psalm 25:4–5, "Show me your ways, O LORD, teach me your paths; guide me in your truth and teach me, for you are God my Savior and my hope is in you all day long."

Communicate to God what you need. Focus on his power to give you courage and self- control as you wait for his answer. John 16:13, "But when he, the Spirit of truth, comes, he will guide you into all truth. He will not speak on his own; he will speak only what he hears, and he will tell you what is yet to come."

Our Heavenly Father has promised to be faithful to us. When the circumstances of life confuse us, depend on His Word. Trust his power. Remember Psalm 27:4, "One thing I ask of the LORD, this is what I seek: that I may dwell in the house of the LORD all the days of my life, to gaze upon the beauty of the LORD and to seek him in his temple."

Find out the difference between denying self and self-denial. They are not the same. We observe self-denial when we do without things we crave, but we deny self when we follow Christ in absolute submission. Luke 9:23–24, "Then he said to them all: "If anyone would come after me, he must deny himself and take up his cross daily and follow me. For whoever wants to save his life will lose it, but whoever loses his life for me will save it."

If you want to have a friend, then you need to be a friend. Look for someone who is as lonely as you are. It is a great place to start. Isaiah 40:11, "He tends his flock like a shepherd: He gathers the lambs in his arms and carries them close to his heart; he gently leads those that have young."

You will never get yesterday back; determine that you will never forget the value of each day. Psalm 21:13, "Be exalted, O Lord, in your strength; we will sing and praise your might."

Stop blaming your bad day on everyone else. The outcome of any terrible situation is up to you, so decide today to be victorious, not a victim. Isaiah 12:2, "Surely God is my salvation; I will trust and not be afraid. The Lord, the Lord, is my strength and my song; he has become my salvation."

It is a trick. Do not give in to fear; sing a song as loud as you can. God is very near. Isaiah 41:10, "So do not fear, for I am with you; do not be dismayed, for I am your God. I will strengthen you and help you; I will uphold you with my righteous right hand."

Just like you trust your parents to meet your needs, you must also learn to trust and depend on Jesus so that you can understand his love, and be satisfied with his plan so that he will be glorified. John 6:35, "Then Jesus declared, "I am the bread of life. He who comes to me will never go hungry, and he who believes in me will never be thirsty."

Sports

Stay focused. Keep alert. Don't drop your smiles into the dirt. Play hard; play fair. Remember the Lord is everywhere. 1 Corinthians 9:27, "No, I beat my body and make it my slave so that after I have preached to others, I myself will not be disqualified for the prize."

Relax. Keep your eye on the ball and your heart in the game even if you do not place, your attitude will gain great fame. Proverbs 2:11, "Discretion will guard you, understanding will watch over you, to deliver you from the way of evil."

Jesus puts people in our lives to instruct and to guide. In sports those people would be the coaches. Listen, pay attention; they have something to say. Isaiah 30:21, "Whether you turn to the right or to the left, your ears will hear a voice behind you, saying, "This is the way; walk in it."

Do you want to be triumphant today? Then you must treat others the way you want to be treated. Suppress your desire to be selfish, and turn every encounter with others into a positive experience. Ephesians 4:32, "Be kind and compassionate to one another, forgiving each other, just as in Christ God forgave you."

Comparison is the root of all feelings of inadequacy. The second you start comparing others' muscle to your limitations, your self-esteem starts to crumble. 2 Corinthians 10:12, "We do not dare to classify or compare ourselves with some who commend themselves. When they measure themselves by themselves and compare themselves with themselves, they are not wise."

Your worth does not depend on your rank. You are more valuable than all the money in the world simply because God gave you that value. This is a true fact. It doesn't change by the way someone may treat you. *You are valuable.* Colossians 2:10, "And you have been given fullness in Christ, who is the head over every power and authority."

Strength

Our focus must be on God himself, his power, and his strength, not on our own. Exodus 15:2, "The LORD is my strength and my song; he has become my salvation. He is my God, and I will praise him, my father's God, and I will exalt him."

God has a plan for your life, but on the other hand, so does Satan. Remember where your strength comes from. 2 Samuel 22:31–33, "As for God, his way is perfect; the word of the LORD is flawless. He is a shield for all who take refuge in him. For who is God besides the LORD? And who is the Rock except our God? It is God who arms me with strength and makes my way perfect."

When no one else seems to care or understand just remember to go to God, his line is never busy. He will always understand. Luke 10:27 He answered: "Love the Lord your God with all your heart and with all your soul and with all your strength and with all your mind'; and, 'Love your neighbor as yourself.'"

When the whole world is falling apart around you, God can put it back together. Psalm 29:11, "The LORD gives strength to his people; the LORD blesses his people with peace."

Toys, clothes and cars can tear up and get old. When the wind blows it away, the fire burns it up, or the water washes it away, God will still be around ready to show His power. Psalm 33:16–17, "No king is saved by the size of his army; no warrior escapes by his great strength. A horse is a vain hope for deliverance; despite all its great strength it cannot save."

When you think your life is terrible, sing and praise God; your troubles will be bearable. Psalm 59:16–17, "But I will sing of your strength, in the morning I will sing of your love; for you are my fortress, my refuge in times of trouble. O my Strength, I sing praise to you; you, O God, are my fortress, my loving God."

Remember all that God has brought you through and taught you in the process. Tell someone else. It will grow your trust and theirs. Psalm 73:28, "But as for me, it is good to be near God. I have made the Sovereign LORD my refuge; I will tell of all your deeds."

There are days that everything goes wrong. In those stressful times remember that God is still in control and can still calm your spirit. Ask him to. Psalm 89:8–9, "O LORD God Almighty, who is like you? You are mighty, O LORD, and your faithfulness surrounds you. You rule over the surging sea; when its waves mount up, you still them."

When you're freaking out because you don't know how things will turn out...pause. Remember the outcome was decided long before this morning. Isaiah 25:1, "O LORD, you are my God; I will exalt you and praise your name, for in perfect faithfulness you have done marvelous things, things planned long ago."

Do you need a friend to lend a hand? Keep in mind the answers are in God's Word; it is timeless wisdom. Isaiah 33:5–6, "The LORD is exalted, for he dwells on high; he will fill Zion with justice and righteousness. He will be the sure foundation for your times, a rich store of salvation and wisdom and knowledge; the fear of the LORD is the key to this treasure."

If you're stressed out, what do you suppose people are doing that don't have the King of the universe on their side? You're on the winning team, act like a winner. The way you respond to anxiety will be a superb demonstration of your faith. Isaiah 35:3–4, "Strengthen the feeble hands, steady the knees that give way; say to those with fearful hearts, Be strong, do not fear; your God will come, he will come with vengeance; with divine retribution he will come to save you."

Twinkle, twinkle, little star, I know God will not go far. Watching me from heaven above, I speak his name. I feel his love. Isaiah 40:26, "Lift your eyes and look to the heavens: Who created all these? He who brings out the starry host one by one, and calls them each by name. Because of his great power and mighty strength, not one of them is missing."

When will you ever figure out what my love is all about? That cold, hard idol you hold in your hand will never give you the freedom that you demand. Isaiah 43:10–11, "You are my witnesses," declares the LORD, "and my servant whom I have chosen, so that you may know and believe me and understand that I am he. Before me no god was formed, nor will there be one after me."

My way is perfect; your way is not working. I can see the imperfections, and I know you need directions. Isaiah 48:17, "This is what the LORD says—your Redeemer, the Holy One of Israel: "I am the LORD your God, who teaches you what is best for you, who directs you in the way you should go."

What I really need from you right now is cooperation. This kicking and screaming has got to stop. I have things under control. Give me a chance. I can give people ideas and direction, not only that, I never even went to bed last night, so I'm still ahead of you in the "got it together" area. Isaiah 55:8–9, "For my thoughts are not your thoughts, neither are your ways my ways, declares the LORD. As the heavens are higher than the earth, so are my ways higher than your ways and my thoughts than your thoughts."

If you assume you cannot count on God, maybe you should think again. Don't put God in human terms. He is a mystery. 1 Corinthians 1:25, "For the foolishness of God is wiser than man's wisdom, and the weakness of God is stronger than man's strength."

It is good sometimes to get up on the table and look at life from a different perspective. Ask God to show you if you are missing something that he is trying to show you. Be more aware of his presence. Isaiah 40:30–31, "Even youths grow tired and weary, and young men stumble and fall; but those who hope in the LORD will renew their strength. They will soar on wings like eagles; they will run and not grow weary, they will walk and not be faint."

Remember that all you are comes from God; he is the provider of all things. 1 Peter 4:10, "Each one should use whatever gift he has received to serve others, faithfully administering God's grace in its various forms."

Yes it is true. God is in the halls at school, and he is watching you. 2 Chronicles 16:9, "For the eyes of the LORD range throughout the earth to strengthen those whose hearts are fully committed to him."

The same power that raised Christ from the dead is the same power that Jesus offers to you. Plug it in. I promise it will be more satisfying than plugging in the hair dryer. Ephesians 3:16–17, "I pray that out of his glorious riches he may strengthen you with power through his Spirit in your inner being, so that Christ may dwell in your hearts through faith."

It is the Lord that you must fear, not other people, and not your peers. The Lord is the one with awesome power; he will come to your aid regardless of the hour. 2 Timothy 4:17, "But the Lord stood at my side and gave me strength, so that through me the message might be fully proclaimed and all the Gentiles might hear it. And I was delivered from the lion's mouth."

Commit this to memory and say it when you are afraid. God will always be with you and will lead you on your way. Hebrews 13:5–6, God has said, "Never will I leave you; never will I forsake you." So we say with confidence, 'The Lord is my helper; I will not be afraid. What can man do to me?'"

Two ways to know you can trust in God: he has not failed you yet. He has been with you in good times and bad. I John 4:10, "This is love: not that we loved God, but that he loved us and sent his Son as an atoning sacrifice for our sins."

We were never promised a life of ease. God promised he would be with us and help us. Don't get the two confused. John 16:33 "I have told you these things, so that in me you may have peace. In this world you will have trouble. But take heart! I have overcome the world."

He is aware of your loneliness, fear and exhaustion. Only he can meet that need because he is your heavenly father. Do not be anxious. Psalm 23:4, "Even though I walk through the valley of the shadow of death, I will fear no evil, for you are with me; your rod and your staff, they comfort me."

If the nighttime makes you fear, look at the stars that have been in the sky for years. Psalm 56:3–4, "When I am afraid, I will trust in you. In God, whose word I praise, in God I trust; I will not be afraid. What can mortal man do to me?"

We must be able to take a stand against false doctrine and godless practices. We must separate our selves from them. This must be based on the Bible and not personal opinion or a carnal spirit. Isaiah 46:8–9, "Remember this, fix it in mind, take it to heart, you rebels. Remember the former things, those of long ago; I am God, and there is no other; I am God, and there is none like me."

The more we focus on his truth the more we experience abundant life. It is a minute-by-minute relationship. Colossians 3:2–3, "Set your minds on things above, not on earthly things. For you died, and your life is now hidden with Christ in God."

ABC's

A is for action always on the go. Share the love of Jesus with all the friends you know. Acts 4:12, "Salvation is found in no one else, for there is no other name under heaven given to men by which we must be saved."

B is for believing that Jesus is God's son. He will never break a promise, not even one. Numbers 23:19, "God is not a man, that he should lie, nor a son of man, that he should change his mind. Does he speak and then not act? Does he promise and not fulfill?"

C is for comparison, a thing you should not do. There will always be someone who believes they are better than you. Matthew 5:9, "Blessed are the peacemakers, for they will be called sons of God."

D is for doing kind things for others; you can start at home with your sisters and brothers. Romans 12:10, "Be devoted to one another in brotherly love. Honor one another above yourselves."

E is for eyes to see what God can do. What you find out might surprise you. Luke 11:34, "Your eye is the lamp of your body. When your eyes are good, your whole body also is full of light. But when they are bad, your body also is full of darkness."

F is for firm. Stand tall and don't back down, remember the chance to sin is always around. Genesis 4:7, "Sin is crouching at your door; it desires to have you, but you must master it."

G is for the good gifts from our Father above. Every single day he showers us with love. James 1:17, "Every good and perfect gift is from above, coming down from the Father…"

H is for help. Are you ever in trouble? Call to God, he will be there on the double. Jeremiah 32:27, "I am the LORD, the God of all mankind. Is anything too hard for me?"

I is for interest. God is interested in you! There is something special he wants you to do. Psalm 138:8, "The Lord will fulfill his purpose for me; your love, O Lord, endures forever- do not abandon the works of your hands."

J is for joy; you can share some with your friends. You do it by laughing, and giggles and grins. Proverbs 15:30, "A cheerful look brings joy to the heart."

K is for keeping your mind on Christ. This won't be hard to do, just think of all the good things he has done for you. Isaiah 26:3, "You will keep in perfect peace him whose mind is steadfast, because he trusts in you."

L is for love; God will always love you, no matter what. 1 John 3:16, "This is how we know what love is: Jesus Christ laid down his life for us."

M is for mercy; God's free gift to all; his forgiveness will work if on his name you call. Psalm 51:1, "Have mercy on me, O God, according to your unfailing love: according to your great compassion blot out my transgression."

N is for need. Some days they are big needs, other days they are small. Either way, God can satisfy them all. Isaiah 58:11, "The Lord will guide you always, he will satisfy your needs."

O is for obey; this is something you must do if you expect God to take care of you. Psalm 119:4, "...you have laid down precepts that are to be fully obeyed."

P is for peace that comes from God's love. John 14:27, "Peace I leave with you; my peace I give to you. I do not give to you as the world gives. Do not let your heart be troubled and do not be afraid."

Q is for quiet—you don't have to be loud. It takes a strong person to listen without a sound. Isaiah 30:15, "...in quietness and trust is your strength."

R is for repent; it means stop doing wrong. Ask God to forgive you. Don't wait to long. 1 John 1:9, "If we confess our sins, he is faithful and just and will forgive our sins and purify us from all unrighteousness."

S is for speech; keep it sweet and clean. Never ever say anything mean. Matthew 12:36, "But I tell you that men will have to give account on the day of judgment for every careless word they have spoken."

T is for trust! Faith in the Lord is a must. Psalm 37:3, "Trust in the Lord and do good."

U is for understanding. God has a special plan for you. If life seems confusing, ask him what to do. Ephesians 5:17, "Therefore do not be foolish, but understand what the Lord's will is."

V is for victory it is our battle cry. You cannot win without Jesus, don't even try. 1 John 5:4–5, "This is the victory that has overcome the world, even our faith. Who is it that overcomes the world? Only he who believes that Jesus is the Son of God."

W is for walk; it is a step we all must take; to go the wrong direction would be a serious mistake. Proverbs 4:27, "Do not swerve to the right or to the left; keep your foot from evil."

X is for example following his lead. You won't be disappointed if his commandments you heed. 1Corinthians 11:1, "Follow the example of Christ."

Y is for young. That of course would be you. Let your life be a blessing that God can use. 1Timothy 4:12 "Don't let anyone look down on you, because you are young, but set an example for the believers in speech in life in love, in faith and in purity."

Z is for zeal: persistent devotion for the cause. Remember why we are fighting ... there is no time to pause. Proverbs 23:17, " ... always be zealous for the fear of the Lord."

Always

God is not tired of you and your problems. He came to be your constant helper and guide. Deuteronomy 5:29, "Oh, that their hearts would be inclined to fear me and keep all my commands always, so that it might go well with them and their children forever!"

In the life of a follower of Jesus, we recommend that you do not take a day off. Keep your seat belts fastened and your earphones plugged in. You may be headed for some slight turbulence. Thank you for walking in the truth, and thank you for being available to the cause. Deuteronomy 11:1, "Love the LORD your God and keep his requirements, his decrees, his laws and his commands always."

There will always be someone who will tell you that you can get by without praying or reading your Bible daily. Don't believe it. Remind yourself of this important message from the Father. Deuteronomy 28:13, "The LORD will make you the head, not the tail. If you pay attention to the commands of the LORD your God that I give you this day and carefully follow them, you will always be at the top, never at the bottom."

Happy lunchtime. This is an important day and just like all the others, I am holding the whole world in my hands. After all these years, I am still not tired and am actually quite capable of handling whatever comes your way today, so sit back and relax and breathe for heaven's sake. P.S. I am the strong one who loves you the most. 1 Chronicles 16:11, "Look to the LORD and his strength; seek his face always."

Don't freak when things get messed up. Instead repeat to yourself, "No matter what happens God is not surprised and he is always working for my good." Psalms 16:8, "I have set the LORD always before me. Because he is at my right hand, I will not be shaken."

When you are in turmoil or just so upset you can't see straight, the best thing to do is to tell God how much you love him. It is an instant attitude changer. Psalm 34:1, "I will extol the LORD at all times; his praise will always be on my lips."

When you are in trouble, call on your heavenly Father to help you. He is just a prayer away. Psalm 40:11, "Do not withhold your mercy from me, O LORD; may your love and your truth always protect me."

The best remedy for depression is praise. Give thanks to God in good times and bad. Psalm 40:16, "May all who seek you rejoice and be glad in you; may those who love your salvation always say, The LORD be exalted!"

When things are not going well, that does not mean that you have been bad or that you are being punished. Sometimes life is just *hard*. This is when you can get real excited that God is always near. Psalm 71:14, "But as for me, I will always have hope; I will praise you more and more."

Come just as you are. God loves you and will hold on to you no matter what. He will not let go of our hand … *ever*. Psalm 73:23, "Yet I am always with you; you hold me by my right hand."

The Lord our God is committed to meeting every need that we have, whether it is spiritual or material. Remember that he gives food to birds, and he likes you better than birds. Psalms 68:28, "Summon your power, O God; show us your strength, O God, as you have done before."

What is the source of your strength? Is it your money, car or brains? No, no the source of your strength is the Lord. Jeremiah 17:8, "He will be like a tree planted by the water that sends out its roots by the stream. It does not fear when heat comes; its leaves are always green. It has no worries in a year of drought and never fails to bear fruit."

God's timing is never early and never late. He will not delay in helping you. Keep praying and trusting. That is how you grow to be who God wants you to be. Luke 18:1, "Then Jesus told his disciples a parable to show them that they should always pray and not give up."

Do not panic if you do not see results. God is always awake and always working. He does not take a day off. How do you believe those stars get out at night, and who do you believe creates the sunrise? John 5:17, "Jesus said to them, My Father is always at his work to this very day, and I, too, am working."

When going though difficult times remember God's grace is sufficient to meet your need, regardless of the situation. 2 Corinthians 2:14, "But thanks be to God, who always leads us in triumphal procession in Christ and through us spreads everywhere the fragrance of the knowledge of him."

Just remember that as a secret agent there is a little danger involved. But oh, consider the places you will go, and the weapons you have at your disposal. 2 Corinthians 4:10–11, "We always carry around in our body the death of Jesus, so that the life of Jesus may also be revealed in our body. For we who are alive are always being given over to death for Jesus' sake, so that his life may be revealed in our mortal body."

When someone encourages you with his or her actions, say a special prayer for him or her. Ephesians 6:18, "And pray in the Spirit on all occasions with all kinds of prayers and requests. With this in mind, be alert and always keep on praying for all the saints."

Never miss an opportunity to keep your mouth shut. Proverbs 17:28, "Even a fool is thought wise if he keeps silent, and discerning if he holds his tongue."

Just when you assume you are the only one who understands ... someone will surprise you ... they understand too. Your efforts are not fruitless after all. 2 Thessalonians 1:3, "We ought always to thank God for you, brothers, and rightly so, because your faith is growing more and more, and the love every one of you has for each other is increasing."

As soon as you feel alone, talk to the one friend who knows everything about you and still believes you are the absolute best. Jesus is always ready to hear your voice. Hebrews 7:25, "Therefore he is able to save completely those who come to God through him, because he always lives to intercede for them."

We must never forget the treasure we have in our hearts. Someone always wants to know the truth. Your mission is to get the truth out! Never underestimate its power. 1 Peter 3:15, "But in your hearts set apart Christ as Lord. Always be prepared to give an answer to everyone who asks you to give the reason for the hope that you have. But do this with gentleness and respect."

Rather than babbling folly, practice silence. Do not be like the fool who is quick with his mouth. Proverbs 10:14, "Wise men store up knowledge, but the mouth of a fool invites ruin."

Store up knowledge, not anger, so when you need it, you can use it. Be discreet when you speak, save some facts for later. Proverbs 12:23, "A prudent man keeps his knowledge to himself, but the heart of fools blurts out folly."

As a believer you were called to lead! Choose your friends with care and do not let anyone lead you where you do not wish to go. Proverbs 12:25–26, "An anxious heart weighs a man down, but a kind word cheers him up. A righteous man is cautious in friendship, but the way of the wicked leads them astray."

It is always right to encourage. Always. Anyone. Everyone. It is a sign of strength and maturity. Proverbs 11:25, "A generous man will prosper; he who refreshes others will himself be refreshed."

No matter what crosses your path, it has been sifted through the hands of God. He will not give you a task for which you are not prepared. Psalm 57:1, "Have mercy on me, O God, have mercy on me, for in you my soul takes refuge. I will take refuge in the shadow of your wings until the disaster has passed."

Stop relying on your feelings. Deal with the facts; stop the devil's attacks. Psalm 9:10, "Those who know your name will trust in you, for you, LORD, have never forsaken those who seek you."

Don't let anyone rain on your parade; trust in his name and you will have it made. Psalm 33:21, "In him our hearts rejoice, for we trust in his holy name."

Jesus understands how you feel because he was with you when it happened. Whatever it was I know he was there. Psalm 62:8, "Trust in him at all times, O people; pour out your hearts to him, for God is our refuge." Selah

Whatever you are going through usually looks better by the morning time. Let the sunrise remind you of God's faithfulness. Psalm 143:8, "Let the morning bring me word of your unfailing love, for I have put my trust in you. Show me the way I should go, for to you I lift up my soul."

We cannot make it on our own. Rely on the Holy Spirit to sustain you. Romans 15:13, "May the God of hope fill you with all joy and peace as you trust in him, so that you may overflow with hope by the power of the Holy Spirit."

Who are you when no one else is looking? My point of course is that someone is always looking. Whoever you really are, be that person all the time. 1 Corinthians 4: 2, "Now it is required that those who have been given a trust must prove faithful."

Old Testament

Don't be a Christian that "comes down" with society. Just because sin is accepted, it doesn't make it right. Raise the standard! Be a blessing that others can experience. Genesis 39:9, "How could I do such a wicked thing and sin against God?"

When you know you need to change, then do it right away. Don't put off till tomorrow what you can change today. Jesus is always with you; he will give you strength—even if the problem really, really, stinks. Why would Pharaoh want to spend one more night with the frogs? Exodus 8:9–10, "Moses said to Pharaoh, 'I leave you the honor of setting the time for me to pray for you and your officials and your people that you and your houses may be rid of the frogs.' 'Tomorrow,' Pharaoh said."

Jesus bought you with his blood. Live your life to honor and please him. Then you will experience real joy. Leviticus 20:7, "'Consecrate yourselves and be holy, because I am the Lord your God." Keep my decrees and follow them. I am the Lord who makes you holy."

So you suppose you have a problem that cannot be solved. You can't think straight and you worry all the time. Put your trust in God. He does not make mistakes. Numbers 11:23, "The Lord answered Moses, Is the Lord's arm too short? You will now see whether or not what I say will come true for you."

We all have choices to make, well really only two. The quality of life you live totally depends on you! Deuteronomy 30:19, "This day I call heaven and earth as witnesses against you that I have set before you life and death, blessings and curses. Now choose life, so that you and your children may live."

Every now and then it is a good idea to take inventory of your life. Throw out what you don't need, clean up what you do, and be faithful to the one true God. Sometimes our schedules just crowd him out of our lives. Joshua 24:14, "Now fear the LORD and serve him with all faithfulness. Throw away the gods your forefathers worshiped beyond the River and in Egypt, and serve the LORD."

The Lord is always working for you. It's the other people who need to worry. Judges 5:31, "So may all your enemies perish, O LORD! But may they who love you be like the sun when it rises in its strength."

Your true character will be revealed when you face difficult circumstances. Make sure your love; loyalty, and devotion always remain true to Christ and his people. Ruth 1:16, "But Ruth replied, Don't urge me to leave you or to turn back from you. Where you go I will go, and where you stay I will stay. Your people will be my people and your God my God."

You can keep some things hidden from your siblings, parents or friends, but just remember this: Jesus is never fooled. Not by motive or action. His vision sees right through your bones. 1 Samuel 2:2–3, "There is no one holy like the LORD; there is no one besides you; there is no Rock like our God. "Do not keep talking so proudly or let your mouth speak such arrogance, for the LORD is a God who knows, and by him deeds are weighed."

Can you imagine the pressure if we could never make a mistake? What a comfort to know that even when we mess up, God can still work to make our ways perfect. There is no one like him. What a great gift to be protected by his shield! (P.S. stay behind the shield) 2 Samuel 22:31, "As for God, his way is perfect; the word of the LORD is flawless. He is a shield for all who take refuge in him."

Sooner or later people are going to disappoint you. They are going to hurt you. They are going to forget about you, because people are not perfect. Give wholehearted devotion to God. Not people. He won't do that. Never has, never will. 1 Kings 8:23, "O LORD, God of Israel, there is no God like you in heaven above or on earth below—you who keep your covenant of love with your servants who continue wholeheartedly in your way."

There are times when the enemy gets way to close. He is right at your heels, ready to suck the life right out of you. That is how Hezekiah felt. He had lots of unwanted company. They were on his doorstep ready to kill him! That is when we have to "sit tight and trust." When it looks like nothing is happening … God is just getting started. 2 Kings 19:35, "That night the angel of the LORD went out and put to death a hundred and eighty-five thousand men in the Assyrian camp. When the people got up the next morning—there were all the dead bodies."

Your job is to stay righteous. Obey God and do what you are told. Leave the results up to him. I am confident you will be pleased with his qualifications. Ask any of his satisfied customers. 1 Chronicles 19:13, "Be strong and let us fight bravely for our people and the cities of our God. The LORD will do what is good in his sight."

Have you ever had a really bad day? Do your best to stay controlled. The devil loves to use those opportunities to embarrass you and ruin your witness. Get your strength from God, not your circumstances. I love you, I am praying for you. You are precious to me. 2 Chronicles 16:9, "For the eyes of the LORD range throughout the earth to strengthen those whose hearts are fully committed to him."

If you are feeling ho-hum and not very motivated to serve God, then picture this: Ezra 8:22, "The gracious hand of our God is on everyone who looks to him, but his great anger is against all who forsake him." How is that for a pick me up!

When you feel sad and blue, repeat to yourself the things that are true. Nehemiah 9:5, "Stand up and praise the LORD your God, who is from everlasting to everlasting. Blessed be your glorious name, and may it be exalted above all blessing and praise."

One of the most courageous acts you can perform is to go against the crowd and do what you know is right. It could save your life … or it could cost you your life. Esther 4:14, "For if you remain silent at this time, relief and deliverance for the Jews will arise from another place, but you and your father's family will perish. And who knows but that you have come to royal position for such a time as this?"

Creation testifies to God's sovereignty and power. The sun, the moon, the stars, and weather are all under his command. There is not a problem that he does not know about. What a marvelous thing that the King of all creation is also your heavenly Father. Job 38:4, "Where were you when I laid the earth's foundation? Tell me, if you understand."

The Lord has a special plan for your life. Part of that plan is for you to obey his laws. These laws are for our good. He made them for our protection. Psalm 119:35–37, "Direct me in the path of your commands, for there I find delight. Turn my heart toward your statutes and not toward selfish gain. Turn my eyes away from worthless things; preserve my life according to your word."

If we store up good thing in our hearts, then good things will come out of our mouths. Be careful what you put in that storage space of the mind! Proverbs 4:23, "Above all else, guard your heart, for it is the wellspring of life."

Have you ever thought about the fact that God made this whole world and everything in it just for us? Yet the more we have the more we want. The world cannot satisfy our needs. That is because he made us for eternity. So, the things of time and space will never satisfy. Only Jesus can satisfy your soul. Ecclesiastes 3:11, "He has made everything beautiful in its time. He has also set eternity in the hearts of men; yet they cannot fathom what God has done from beginning to end."

Don't be discouraged if you don't have a date. Jesus is saving some one to be your mate. Please remember as you wait, our Jesus is never, ever late. He will be the perfect choice for you, he wrote this song to sing to you! Song of Songs 2:13, "Arise, come, my darling; my beautiful one, come with me."

Endurance is what you need to make it through. God is right here waiting to help you. Discipline your body, mind, heart, and soul. Keep your emotions under your control. Stick to your task until it is done. Then when you have finished, relax and have some fun. Isaiah 7:9, "If you do not stand firm in your faith, you will not stand at all."

A responsible person accepts the consequences for their actions. Remember that your choices become your habits, and your habits become your character. Count the cost. Is it worth my time, money, and reputation? Jeremiah 6:16, "This is what the LORD says: Stand at the crossroads and look; ask for the ancient paths, ask where the good way is, and walk in it, and you will find rest for your souls."

Some days are bad; then they keep getting worse. Take comfort in the fact that Jesus has already experienced whatever it is that you are going through. He loves you and will take care of you. Wait and trust in him. Lamentations 3:21–23, "Yet this I call to mind and therefore I have hope: Because of the Lord's great love we are not consumed, for his compassion's never fail. They are new every morning; great is your faithfulness."

People may like to pretend that they have lots of power, and maybe they do to some extent, nonetheless, The Lord is the ultimate power. Some may choose not to believe, but that does not change the facts. Ezekiel 17:24, "All the trees of the field will know that I the LORD bring down the tall tree and make the low tree grow tall. I dry up the green tree and make the dry tree flourish. I the LORD have spoken, and I will do it."

Daniel had already chosen not to defile himself with a worldly lifestyle. It was not a choice that his parents or friends made for him. It was totally between him and GOD. What is your resolve? Are you keeping it? Daniel 1:8, "But Daniel resolved not to defile himself with the royal food and wine, and he asked the chief official for permission not to defile himself this way."

Do you let little problems and irritations "sap your strength?" These situations can detain you from your real goal. Do not be deceived or senseless, but realize who the foreigners are, and do not become involved in their battles. Hosea 7:9–11, "Foreigners sap his strength, but he does not realize it. His hair is sprinkled with gray, but he does not notice. Israel's arrogance testifies against him, but despite all this he does not return to the LORD his God or search for him."

Never forget that God is *for* you. He loves you and you can't do anything to change how he feels about you. Look throughout the whole Bible and you will see the incredible love he has for you and me. He relents (puts off)from sending calamity. Joel 2:13, "Rend your heart and not your garments. Return to the LORD your God, for he is gracious and compassionate, slow to anger and abounding in love, and he relents from sending calamity."

Our God has power and majesty, yet he is easily assessable to you…day or night. Any problem, big or small, that matters to you matters to him. At any given moment he could execute 10,000 angels to come to your aid. That is how important you are to him. Amos 4:13, "He who forms the mountains, creates the wind, and reveals his thoughts to man, he who turns dawn to darkness, and treads the high places of the earth—the LORD God Almighty is his name."

Everyday we face struggles. Let Satan see your commitment to God. You can't have it both ways. Live for God. Obadiah 1:15, "The day of the LORD is near for all nations. As you have done, it will be done to you; your deeds will return upon your own head."

Clinging to possessions or people is a harmful habit. People won't tell you that it is evil, but that is what is kind of scary about it. Get rid of the toys that consume your life and put your relationships in proper order. JOY = Jesus, Others, You. Don't make God do it for you. Jonah 2:8–9, "Those who cling to worthless idols forfeit the grace that could be theirs. But I, with a song of thanksgiving, will sacrifice to you. What I have vowed I will make good. Salvation comes from the LORD."

When you mess up don't make excuses. Your disobedience separates you from the Lord. He longs to forgive you, to hold you in his open arms and comfort you. Say, "I'm sorry" and feel his grace and mercy flood your life. Micah 7:18–19, "Who is a God like you, who pardons sin and forgives the transgression of the remnant of his inheritance? You do not stay angry forever but delight to show mercy. You will again have compassion on us; you will tread our sins underfoot and hurl all our iniquities into the depths of the sea."

When the battle gets tough, remember, Jesus is just getting started. Trust him. Nahum 1:7, "The LORD is good, a refuge in times of trouble. He cares for those who trust in him."

You don't need faith in your faith. You need faith in your God. When you encounter heartache and loss, rejoice in the fact that our Savior is near and will enable you to go on even when you don't believe you can. Habakkuk 3:19, "The Sovereign LORD is my strength; he makes my feet like the feet of a deer, he enables me to go on the heights."

Jesus is faithful. He is worthy of your obedience because he is perfect in all his ways. You can trust him. Zephaniah 3:17, "The LORD your God is with you, he is mighty to save. He will take great delight in you, he will quiet you with his love, he will rejoice over you with singing."

You get to choose the type of life you live. It is not up to your parents, your teachers, or your friends. Only you decide what choices you will make. Remember that you will always reap what your sow. You win or lose by the way you choose. Haggai 2:4, "Be strong, all you people of the land,' declares the LORD, 'and work. For I am with you,' declares the LORD Almighty."

Never, ever give up. Keep on going no matter how weary you are. In the end it will be worth it all. Just keep in mind that the victory celebration is going to be out of this world Zechariah 4:6, "So he said to me, This is the word of the LORD to Zerubbabel: 'Not by might nor by power, but by my Spirit,' says the LORD Almighty."

When you start thinking about how it seems like the losers always win, bear in mind that it is a "short term" victory. Malachi 3:18, "And you will again see the distinction between the righteous and the wicked, between those who serve God and those who do not."

New Testament

Don't follow the crowd. Dare to be different. Be a trend -setter. People who are followers never try new things. Be a leader; lead others to Christ. Matthew 7:14, "But small is the gate and narrow the road that leads to life, and only a few find it."

Christ wants the first part of your day, not the leftovers. How can he work through you if you never go to the meetings? Mark 1:35, "Very early in the morning, while it was still dark, Jesus got up, left the house and went off to a solitary place, where he prayed."

Reaping and sowing was God's idea. Maybe people don't come by and check your fruit on a daily basis, but believe me, when it is time for harvest your good life is going to show through. Luke 6:43- 44, "No good tree bears bad fruit, nor does a bad tree bear good fruit. Each tree is recognized by its own fruit."

A relationship with the living God, the creator of the universe, is absolutely necessary for life. Without him, there is nothing. John 15:5, "I am the vine; you are the branches. If a man remains in me and I in him, he will bear much fruit; apart from me you can do nothing."

Jesus is in the business of changing lives. He uses ordinary people who are sold out to him. If you have been with Jesus, people will recognize the boldness, assurance, and honesty in your life. Acts 4:13, "When they saw the courage of Peter and John and realized that they were unschooled, ordinary men, they were astonished and they took note that these men had been with Jesus."

When you feel like you can't go on, and you do not understand what God is doing in your life, simply depend on him. God is always working for your good. He will give you the strength you need to finish the task. Romans 11:36, "For from him and through him and to him are all things. To him be the glory forever! Amen."

Jesus made you just like you are for his glory. He saved you for a purpose—that you would bring others to Christ. He can work through you, but you have to ask him. Just remember, you can do more with God in an hour than you can by yourself in a lifetime. 1 Corinthians 15:10, "But by the grace of God I am what I am, and his grace to me was not without effect. No, I worked harder than all of them—yet not I, but the grace of God that was with me."

No matter how heavy our load, God is stronger. No matter how dark the day, God shines brighter. No matter how difficult the task, you have not yet resisted to the point of shedding your blood on the cross. The power that raised him from the dead lives inside you every day. Use it. 2 Corinthians 4: 7, "But we have this treasure in jars of clay to show that this all-surpassing power is from God and not from us."

You must carry on. Do not be downcast. Move forward push on. Don't live a day without the power of Jesus. Galatians 5:7–8, "You were running a good race. Who cut in on you and kept you from obeying the truth? That kind of persuasion does not come from the one who calls you."

When I prayed for you this morning, I asked God to give you open eyes to see his glory. I'm never too busy to ask God to give you vigor and bravery and influence. Ephesians 1:18–19, "I pray also that the eyes of your heart may be enlightened in order that you may know the hope to which he has called you, the riches of his glorious inheritance in the saints, and his incomparably great power for us who believe."

You have to make your choices before the situation. Not see the situation, and then make a choice. I am confident of your love for Christ. That is a blessing. You are a very mature believer. Thanks for the sacrifices that you make on a daily basis. Philippians 1: 28, "Then, whether I come and see you or only hear about you in my absence, I will know that you stand firm in one spirit, contending as one man for the faith of the gospel without being frightened in any way by those who oppose you."

Prayer is powerful. Don't leave anything to chance. Ask for God to fill you with spiritual wisdom. Colossians 1:9, "For this reason, since the day we heard about you, we have not stopped praying for you and asking God to fill you with the knowledge of his will through all spiritual wisdom and understanding."

Remember that life as a Christian is an uphill bike ride! I am proud of your progress, stay focused and steady. 1 Thessalonians 4:1, "Finally, brothers, we instructed you how to live in order to please God, as in fact you are living. Now we ask you and urge you in the Lord Jesus to do this more and more."

God has commanded us to share the gospel one on one, rapidly. What is taking you so long to share the truth? 2 Thessalonians 3:1–2, "Finally, brothers, pray for us that the message of the Lord may spread rapidly and be honored, just as it was with you. And pray that we may be delivered from wicked and evil men, for not everyone has faith."

Who you are should be quite plain to others. Always be an example and exhorter of the Lord. Being young is a poor excuse for not being spiritual. 1 Timothy 4:8, "For physical training is of some value, but godliness has value for all things, holding promise for both the present life and the life to come."

We must be emptied, unsoiled and accessible for God to use us. He will secure us, replenish us and use us for his glory. Be discerning and cautious, for you are sanctified. 2 Timothy 2:22, "Flee the evil desires of youth, and pursue righteousness, faith, love and peace, along with those who call on the Lord out of a pure heart."

Salvation is not accomplished by human deeds, but by God's great mercy. Titus 3:4–5, "But when the kindness and love of God our Savior appeared, he saved us, not because of righteous things we had done, but because of his mercy. He saved us through the washing of rebirth and renewal by the Holy Spirit."

Be intentional in sharing your faith. Our world is in serious spiritual crisis. Time is short. Be bold. Philemon 1:6, "I pray that you may be active in sharing your faith, so that you will have a full understanding of every good thing we have in Christ."

We must depend on Jesus just as Jesus depends on his heavenly Father. He has set an example that we must follow. Hebrews 1:3, "The Son is the radiance of God's glory and the exact representation of his being, sustaining all things by his powerful word. After he had provided purification for sins, he sat down at the right hand of the Majesty in heaven."

Keep your focus on God not on your moral strength; rely on God's power. James 1:12, "Blessed is the man who perseveres under trial, because when he has stood the test, he will receive the crown of life that God has promised to those who love him."

If God planned a Savior then we must have needed one. Decide now to set yourself apart from impurity and sin. Instead strive for holiness. 1 Peter 1:14–15, "As obedient children, do not conform to the evil desires you had when you lived in ignorance. But just as he who called you is holy, so be holy in all you do."

God has made everything that we need for salvation obtainable to every person. There are no undisclosed rules you have to follow. All you need is in His Word. 2 Peter 1:4, "He has given us his very great and precious promises, so that through them you may participate in the divine nature and escape the corruption in the world caused by evil desires."

Don't love the world or the things that it offers. Love people. Love our Father. 1 John 2:15, "Do not love the world or anything in the world. If anyone loves the world, the love of the Father is not in him."

You have to love each other. Hate the sin. Not the sinner. 2 John 1:6, "And this is love: that we walk in obedience to his commands. As you have heard from the beginning, His command is that you walk in love."

God calls us to a life of goodness. Not just an occasional kind deed or two, but a lifestyle of service. This is not because you want to make a good impression, but you serve God because you love him. He came to give you eternal life. He died just for you. Can you offer him less? 3 John 1:11, "Dear friends, do not imitate what is evil but what is good. Anyone who does what is good is from God. Anyone who does what is evil has not seen God."

When you see fellow Christians making poor mistakes, encourage them to do right. Don't follow them into sin. Be a source of strength and encouragement. Jude 1:22–23, "Be merciful to those who doubt; snatch others from the fire and save them; to others show mercy, mixed with fear—hating even the clothing stained by corrupted flesh."

God's power and his holiness continue from eternity past to the eternity yet to come. He is worthy of our praise and worship. Honor him. Revelation 4:11, "You are worthy, our Lord and God, to receive glory and honor and power, for you created all things, and by your will they were created and have their being."

Every Day Life

You have to be an example now, right here among your peers. Let them see you go to God with your fears. Jeremiah 12:5 "If you have raced with men on foot and they have worn you out, how can you compete with horses? If you stumble in safe country, how will you manage in the thickets by the Jordan?"

When your friends are unkind to you, don't just assume they are mad at you. Maybe they had a fight with their sister or brother; maybe they said something ugly to their mother. They need a friend more than you realize. Reach out to them. Galatians 6:9, "Let us not become weary in doing good, for at the proper time we will reap a harvest if we do not give up."

When a roadblock is in your way, don't let it ruin your day. Run the race with grace and ease. It is the Father you must please. Hebrews 12:1, "Therefore, since we are surrounded by such a great cloud of witnesses, let us throw off everything that hinders and the sin that so easily entangles, and let us run with perseverance the race marked out for us."

Have you seen grace? It might not be seen in different colors, but the real question is: can others see God's grace in you by your actions and attitudes? 2 Corinthians 5:21, "God made him who had no sin to be sin for us, so that in him we might become the righteousness of God."

When you let other people control you, it only leads to regret. So be led by the Lord Most High, then you will not fret. Proverbs 3:26, "For the Lord will be your confidence and will keep your foot from being snared."

You're walking down the hall, on your way to class. You start to think, *I just don't care. I hate these clothes that I have to wear. I don't like my lunch and I'm not a part of that cool bunch. Look, now someone has stolen my lunch.* Psalm 20:1, "May the Lord answer you when you are in distress; may the name of the God of Jacob protect you."

The teacher says the report is due. The boy you like just won't notice you. Today your hair-do totally stinks. At least you can say, "The Lord is my strength." Luke 11:9–10, "So I say to you: Ask and it will be given to you; seek and you will find; knock and the door will be opened to you. For everyone who asks receives; he who seeks finds; and to him who knocks, the door will be opened."

Some days are good some days are bad. But remember, God always has something to say to you. Be ready to hear, He is always very near. Proverbs 29:25, "Fear of man will prove to be a snare, but whoever trust in the Lord is kept safe."

What gives you joy? How do you spend time? What do you fill your life with? Jesus wants to be a part of everything you do. He loves you and he knows you. Jeremiah 33:3, "Call to me and I will answer you and tell you great and unsearchable things you do not know."

There are some days that we all feel blue. Those days it is hard to believe God's Word is true. Recognize that it is only a feeling or your day will keep on reeling. Proverbs 30:5, "Every word of God is flawless; he is a shield to those who take refuge in him."

When you come to a losing situation and there seems to be no way out, you may get cross and angry or maybe even pout. Step back and remember what God's power is all about. Matthew 14:27, "But Jesus immediately said to them: "Take courage! It is I. Don't be afraid."

Early in the morning or the middle of the night, you got to worrying about your life and if things would ever be right. That's when you remembered, "The Lord is my light." John 8:12, "When Jesus spoke again to the people, he said, "I am the light of the world. Whoever follows me will never walk in darkness, but will have the light of life."

Don't let other people bother you. Do what is right, even when it is tough. That is the best way to prove God is strong. Hebrews 10:35–36, "So do not throw away your confidence; it will be richly rewarded. You need to persevere so that when you have done the will of God, you will receive what he has promised."

God knew you would get sick of it all, he knew that you would stumble and fall. He is right beside you waiting for you to call. He wants to come and give you hope, so don't just wait and try to cope. Isaiah 40:30–31, "Even youth grow tired and weary, and young men stumble and fall; but those who wait on the Lord will renew their strength. They will soar on wings like eagles, they will run and not grow weary, they will walk and not faint."

When a bolt from the blue comes and surprises you, don't forget to call on Jesus; He has already said this to you. Joshua 1:9, "Have I not commanded you? Be strong and courageous. Do not be terrified; do not be discouraged, for the Lord your God will be with you wherever you go."

Remember that whatever happens today, you can handle it. God is not surprised and he's ready to intervene. Give him a call. That's 1–800-God-cares. Deuteronomy 29:29, "The secret things belong to the LORD our God, but the things revealed belong to us and to our children forever, that we may follow all the words of this law."

Think about what you do, because somebody is always watching you. Ephesians 5: 15–16, "Be very careful, then, how you live—not as unwise but wise, making the most of every opportunity, because the days are evil"

Suffer now because of what you believe, just remember that this world, someday we will leave. Romans 8:18, "I consider that our present sufferings are not worth comparing with the glory that will be revealed in us."

Faith, hope, and love is more than a song. It is a gift from God that will last all day long. 1 Corinthians 13:13, "And now these three remain, faith, hope and love. But the greatest of these is love."

There is something you must never do. Never, ever, play with sin; this is a battle you cannot win. 1 Corinthians 10:13, "No temptation has seized you except what is common to man. And God is faithful; he will not let you be tempted beyond what you can bear. But when you are tempted, he will also provide a way out so that you can stand up under it."

Some days if you feel sad, remember the best bath you ever had. That of course would be the day that Jesus washed your sin away. 2 Corinthians 5:17, "Therefore, if anyone is in Christ he is a new creation: the old has gone, the new has come."

Dwell in the shelter the Lord has built for you. His loving arms will give you strength as he carries you. Psalm 91:1–2, "He who dwells in the shelter of the Most High will rest in the shadow of the Almighty. I will say of the LORD, "He is my refuge and my fortress, my God, in whom I trust."

You have a precious treasure that you need to share; it is the gospel of Jesus Christ. Tell someone that God cares. Romans 1:16, "I am not ashamed of the gospel, because it is the power of God for the salvation of everyone who believes: first for the Jew, then for the Gentile."

The thing that makes the difference in you and in me is that we have the love of Christ for eternity. Romans 5:5, "And hope does not disappoint us, because God has poured out his love into our hearts by the Holy Spirit, whom he has given us."

Walk in holiness in all you do. Keep remembering that sin has no hold on you. Ask to be forgiven, and then start each day fresh and new. Romans 8:1, "Therefore, there is now no condemnation for those who are in Christ Jesus."

Every single morning that you get out of bed, you must make a choice in your head. Walk in the Spirit, walk in the light, and set your mind on what is right. Romans 8:5, "Those who live according to the sinful nature have their minds set on what that nature desires; but those who live in accordance with the Spirit have their minds set on what the Spirit desires."

It should make you glad to see that God always has a plan, even if you fail to understand. Your name is written on the palm of his hand. He is not surprised at what you are going through. His power will enable you. Isaiah 49:16, "See, I have engraved you on the palms of my hands; your walls are ever before me."

Whenever you want to quit, and you believe life is too hard remember Jesus, he is the one who is scarred. Romans 8:31–32, "What, then, shall we say in response to this? If God is for us, who can be against us?"

Holiness

The greatness and glory of God is continually at our disposal, but we must first confess our sins. Psalm 66:18–20, "If I had cherished sin in my heart, the Lord would not have listened; but God has surely listened and heard my voice in prayer. Praise be to God, who has not rejected my prayer or withheld his love from me!"

Do not doubt that God is able. Remembering this will make you stable. Isaiah 59:1–2, "Surely the arm of the LORD is not too short to save, nor his ear too dull to hear. But your iniquities have separated you from your God; your sins have hidden his face from you, so that he will not hear."

The Lord longs to be gracious to us, remember that you are his favorite. Do not let pride stand in the way of enjoying a perfectly wonderful day. 2 Chronicles 7:14, "If my people, who are called by my name, will humble themselves and pray and seek my face and turn from their wicked ways, then will I hear from heaven and will forgive their sin and will heal their land."

Who is a righteous man? One who keeps his wrongs confessed so that our God can bless and bless. James 5:16, "Therefore confess your sins to each other and pray for each other so that you may be healed. The prayer of a righteous man is powerful and effective."

Transformation comes through living by the spirit, not by relying on our own abilities and strength. 2 Corinthians 5:14–15, "For Christ's love compels us, because we are convinced that one died for all, and therefore all died.

And he died for all, that those who live should no longer live for themselves but for him who died for them and was raised again."

Our confidence as we live each day is not in what others do or say. The strength we find to make it through comes from our Lord, who is faithful and true. 1 John 3:3, "Everyone who has this hope in him purifies himself, just as he is pure."

How people respond to you is not important, but how you respond to them could matter in eternity. Are you peaceful? Are you holy? Can people see God in you?? Hebrews 12:14, "Make every effort to live in peace with all men and to be holy; without holiness no one will see the Lord."

God wants us to be buff it is true, are you tough in life or is it tough on you? 1 Peter 4:17, "For it is time for judgment to begin with the family of God; and if it begins with us, what will the outcome be for those who do not obey the gospel of God?"

I have never heard anyone say, "I'm sorry I spent time with God today." Hosea 10:12, "Sow for yourselves righteousness, reap the fruit of unfailing love, and break up your unplowed ground; for it is time to seek the LORD, until he comes and showers righteousness on you."

It does not matter if your lies are black or white; give Jesus your sin and be clean by tonight. Isaiah 1:18, "Come now, let us reason together," says the LORD. "Though your sins are like scarlet, they shall be as white as snow; though they are red as crimson, they shall be like wool."

The more time you spend with God the more you become like him. So what are you afraid of? Becoming more like God? What is so wrong with that? James 4:8, "Come near to God and he will come near to you. Wash your hands, you sinners, and purify your hearts, you double-minded."

When God prompts us of the sin in our lives it is because he cannot stand for our fellowship with him to be broken. The longer you put it off, the harder it is. Psalms 103:11–12, "For as high as the heavens are above the earth, so great is his love for those who fear him; as far as the east is from the west, so far has he removed our transgressions from us."

Allow God to put the spotlight of purity on your life. Just a little bit of sin goes a long, long way. Undetected it can eat your life away. Psalms 139:23–24, "Search me, O God, and know my heart; test me and know my anxious thoughts. See if there is any offensive way in me, and lead me in the way everlasting."

When your feelings rule your life you will live with pain and strife. When you die to sin each day you will walk in his perfect way. John 12:25, "The man who loves his life will lose it, while the man who hates his life in this world will keep it for eternal life."

When your life gets dry and weak, go to God's Word, allow him to speak. Colossians 2:6–7, "So then, just as you received Christ Jesus as Lord, continue to live in him, rooted and built up in him, strengthened in the faith as you were taught, and overflowing with thankfulness."

Relinquish that sin that you find yourself in. To pretend it is not there will only cause grief and despair. Proverbs 28:13, "He who conceals his sins does not prosper, but whoever confesses and renounces them finds mercy."

Determine the lies that you believe, do not allow memories to deceive. Set your mind on what is right. 2 Corinthians 10:3–5, "We demolish arguments and every pretension that sets itself up against the knowledge of God, and we take captive every thought to make it obedient to Christ."

Christmas

"Hark the herald angels sing, glory to the new born king!" That song in my head will always ring. Then, I remember, if that is the song that my heart must sing, I must in turn give him everything. He is my King. John 1:1–2, "In the beginning was the Word, and the Word was with God and the Word was God. He was with God in the beginning."

"O little town of Bethlehem, how still we see thee lie, above the deep and dreamless sleep, the silent stars go by." Luke 2:4, "So Joseph also went up from the town of Nazareth in Galilee to Judea, to Bethlehem..." While they were there the baby was born.

"Away in the manger, no crib for a bed, the little Lord Jesus lay down his sweet head, the stars in the sky look down where he lay, the little Lord Jesus asleep on the hay." Luke 2:7, "She wrapped him in cloths and placed him in a manger, because there was no room for him in the inn."

"It came upon a midnight clear this glorious song of old, from angels bending near the earth to touch their harps of gold..." Luke 2:14, "Glory to God in the highest, and on earth peace to men on whom his favor rests."

"Silent night Holy night, all is calm, all is bright..." Have you seen the blessed Savior tonight? Luke 2:11–12, "Today in the town of David a Savior has been born to you; he is Christ the Lord. This will be a sign to you; you will find a baby wrapped in cloths and lying in a manger."

This gift was the greatest gift that the world has ever known; it was God's love. Luke 2: 13–14, "Suddenly a great company of the heavenly host appeared with the angel, praising God and saying, Glory to God in the highest, and on earth peace to men on whom his favor rest."

"Go tell it on the mountain over the hills and everywhere. Go tell it on the mountain that Jesus Christ is born." Luke 2:15, "When the angels had left then and gone into heaven, the shepherds said to one another, Let's go to Bethlehem and see this thing that has happened, which the Lord has told us about."

"The first noel the angel did say was to certain poor shepherds in fields as they lay, keeping their sheep, on a cold winter's night that was so deep. Noel...." Luke 2:16–18, "they hurried off and found Mary and Joseph, and the baby, who was lying in the manger. When they had seen him, they spread the word concerning what had been told them about this child, and all who heard it were amazed at what the shepherds said to them."

"O come let us adore him, Christ the Lord." What does that really mean? We sing it every Christmas, but if Christ is really Lord, the one true and living God, then our values, goals, desires, and habits should point to that. Isaiah 9:6, "For to us a child is born, to us a son is given, and the government will be on his shoulders. And he will be called Wonderful Counselor, Mighty God, Everlasting Father, Prince of Peace."

"Angels from the realms of glory wing your flight or all the earth, ye who sang creations story now proclaim Messiah's birth." Revelations 15:3–4, "Great and marvelous are your deeds, Lord God Almighty. Just and true are your ways, King of the Ages. Who will not fear you, O Lord, and bring Glory to your name? For you alone are holy. All nations will come and worship you, for your righteous acts have been revealed."

"We three kings of orient are bearing gifts we came from afar." We just had trouble keeping up with the star. We could not travel light and ended up in a fight; then Jesus appeared to us that very night. Matthew 2:2, "Where is the one who has been born king of the Jews? We saw his star in the east and have come to worship him."

"O come all you faithful, joyful and triumphant, O come ye, O come ye to Bethlehem, come and behold him born the king of angels …" Jeremiah 29:13, "You will seek me and find me when you seek me with all your heart."

"Joy to the world the Lord has come. Let heaven and nature sing, let heaven and nature sing." Luke 2:29–31, "Sovereign Lord, as you have promised, you now dismiss your servant in peace. For my eyes have seen your salvation, which you have prepared in the sight of all people, a light for revelation to the Gentiles and for glory to your people Israel."

Conclusion

Our homes and families will only be as strong as the individuals inside. Acknowledge what needs to be tweaked in your family or just take some of these ideas and customize them to your own home. The whole point of this book is to awaken your heart and mind to the awesome power of God and family. Our homes do not need to be the same, but they should be centered on God's Word. Use these or other ideas that God gives you to build a firm scriptural foundation for your home.

Perhaps you believe that no one understands your specific family or situation. Maybe the anguish of criticism and defeat from co-workers or family members has left you overwhelmed and powerless. When the bleakness of our circumstances control our thoughts and actions, we can become unreasonable.

Daily we choose what we let into our hearts and influence our lives. What does the heavenly Father want you to leave behind? Are your beliefs in line with the truth of God's Word? To remove the discouragement we must know the truth. The choices that you make become your habits and your habits become your character. You cannot teach or lead your children somewhere that you have never been. You cannot ask them to embrace the truth of God's Word if you do not live your life in victory. Our relationship with the Father will control how we respond to life. Lack of prayer and communion with God suggest that we have forgotten who has power over the daily hardship and hassles that we face everyday.

Stop saying you don't have time to read the Bible or pray. You can read it any time of the day or night and in any order that you want. When you spend time with God, he will search your heart and it improve your hearing. He cannot fill a dirty vessel or an unyielding heart. You must plan to put Jesus in the center of your troubles. When we say His Word we become stronger. When we act out of control and lose our cool our family life is disrupted and awkward. This is not rocket science. Still pride and frustration keep us from saying, "I'm sorry, or "let's try that again."

What most people have is not the quality of life that our Savoir died to give us. He wants the atmosphere in our home to be inviting and pleasant. There will be days we don't get along but they should be brief and not last for days and days. Fix it. Yes it will be uncomfortable, but it isn't like your having the best time anyway. Whether you live alone or with ten people, the atmosphere should reflect his presence.

What do you do now? Ask God. This is his plan. Deuteronomy 6:5–9, "Love the LORD your God with all your heart and with all your soul and with all your strength. These commandments that I give you today are to be upon your hearts. Impress them on your children. Talk about them when you sit at home and when you walk along the road, when you lie down and when you get up. Tie them as symbols on your hands and bind them on your foreheads. Write them on the doorframes of your houses and on your gates." His plan is for your home to be just like this. With his help it can happen.

Joshua 1:8, "Do not let this Book of the Law depart from your mouth; meditate on it day and night, so that you may be careful to do everything written in it. Then you will be prosperous and successful."